D0908995

# Slavery Through the Ages

# Other titles in the World History series

# Slavery Through the Ages

Don Nardo

**LUCENT BOOKS**

*A part of Gale, Cengage Learning*

Detroit • New York • San Francisco • New Haven, Conn • Waterville, Maine • London

**LIBRARY OF CONGRESS CATALOGING-IN-PUBLICATION DATA**

Nardo, Don, 1947-
  Slavery through the ages / by Don Nardo.
      pages cm. -- (World history)
  Includes bibliographical references and index.
  ISBN 978-1-4205-0860-4 (hardcover)
  1. Slavery--History. 2. Slave trade--History. I. Title.
  HT861.N37 2014
  306.3'62--dc23
                                                                2013038217

Lucent Books
27500 Drake Rd.
Farmington Hills, MI 48331

ISBN-13: 978-1-4205-0860-4
ISBN-10: 1-4205-0860-1

Printed in the United States of America
1 2 3 4 5 6 7 17 16 15 14 13

# Contents

# Foreword

Each year, on the first day of school, nearly every history teacher faces the task of explaining why his or her students should study history. Many reasons have been given. One is that lessons exist in the past from which contemporary society can benefit and learn. Another is that exploration of the past allows us to see the origins of our customs, ideas, and institutions. Concepts such as democracy, ethnic conflict, or even things as trivial as fashion or mores, have historical roots.

Reasons such as these impress few students, however. If anything, these explanations seem remote and dull to young minds. Yet history is anything but dull. And therein lies what is perhaps the most compelling reason for studying history: History is filled with great stories. The classic themes of literature and drama—love and sacrifice, hatred and revenge, injustice and betrayal, adversity and overcoming adversity—fill the pages of history books, feeding the imagination as well as any of the great works of fiction do.

The story of the Children's Crusade, for example, is one of the most tragic in history. In 1212 Crusader fever hit Europe. A call went out from the pope that all good Christians should journey to Jerusalem to drive out the hated Muslims and return the city to Christian control. Heeding the call, thousands of children made the journey. Parents bravely allowed many children to go, and entire communities were inspired by the faith of these small Crusaders. Unfortunately, many boarded ships were captained by slave traders, who enthusiastically sold the children into slavery as soon as they arrived at their destination. Thousands died from disease, exposure, and starvation on the long march across Europe to the Mediterranean Sea. Others perished at sea.

Another story, from a modern and more familiar place, offers a soul-wrenching view of personal humiliation but also the ability to rise above it. Hatsuye Egami was one of 110,000 Japanese Americans sent to internment camps during World War II. "Since yesterday we Japanese have ceased to be human beings," he wrote in his diary. "We are numbers. We are no longer Egamis, but the number 23324. A tag with that number is on every trunk, suitcase and bag. Tags, also, on our breasts." Despite such dehumanizing treatment, most internees worked hard to control their bitterness. They created workable communities inside the camps and demonstrated again and again their loyalty as Americans.

These are but two of the many stories from history that can be found in the pages of the Lucent Books World History series. All World History titles rely on sound research and verifiable evidence, and all give students a clear sense of time, place, and chronology through maps and timelines as well as text.

All titles include a wide range of authoritative perspectives that demonstrate the complexity of historical interpretation and sharpen the reader's critical thinking skills. Formally documented quotations and annotated bibliographies enable students to locate and evaluate sources, often instantaneously via the Internet, and serve as valuable tools for further research and debate.

Finally, Lucent's World History titles present rousing good stories, featuring vivid primary source quotations drawn from unique, sometimes obscure sources such as diaries, public records, and contemporary chronicles. In this way, the voices of participants and witnesses as well as important biographers and historians bring the study of history to life. As we are caught up in the lives of others, we are reminded that we too are characters in the ongoing human saga, and we are better prepared for our own roles.

# Important Dates in the

circa 3300–3000 B.C.
The Sumerians begin building the world's first cities in southern Mesopotamia.

circa 1650 B.C.
A Mesopotamian writing, the *Epic of Atrahasis*, describes slavery among the gods in the ages before the creation of humans.

circa 221 B.C.
Chinese emperor Shih Huang Ti orders the construction of the Great Wall of China.

753 B.C.
Traditional date for the founding of Rome in western Italy.

73–71 B.C.
Years of the famous Roman slave rebellion led by the slave-gladiator Spartacus.

| B.C. 3000 | 2000 | 1000 | A.D. 1000 | 1500 |
|---|---|---|---|---|

circa 419 B.C.
The Athenian orator Antiphon writes about slaves and slavery.

circa 200 B.C.–A.D. 200
The period in which slavery in Roman society reaches its height.

1492
Sailing for the Spanish crown, Italian explorer Christopher Columbus lands in what is now the Caribbean isles, setting in motion European exploitation of the Americas.

A.D. 476
The traditional date for Rome's fall.

circa 1792–1750 B.C.
The Babylonian king Hammurabi issues an extensive law code containing several laws pertaining to slavery.

# History of Slavery

**1619**
Twenty black slaves arrive in Virginia, the first Africans shipped to Britain's North American colonies.

**1807**
Britain and the United States ban the slave trade.

**1776**
Britain's thirteen North American colonies declare their independence, thereby creating the United States.

**1861–1865**
The American Civil War is fought mainly over the issue of slavery and brings about the freeing of the country's black slaves.

| 1600 | 1700 | 1800 | 1900 | 2000 |
|------|------|------|------|------|

**1696**
South Carolina passes the first black codes, designed to keep black people in bondage, in colonial America.

**1939–1945**
World War II draws in dozens of nations and results in the death of more than 50 million people.

**2000**
The United Nations passes the Trafficking Protocol, designed to fight human trafficking and help its victims.

**2001**
Islamic terrorists attack the World Trade Center towers in New York City, setting in motion the so-called War on Terror.

**2011**
The large Internet company Google donates $11.5 million to ongoing efforts to fight human trafficking.

# How Historians Learn About Slavery

In the final years of the twentieth century, archaeologists busily worked to excavate sections of Bigbury Hill in Kent, a county in southeastern England. The partially wooded mound once held a large, sturdy hill fort constructed of packed earth fortified with timber and stone. It was built in about 100 B.C. by the Iron Age Celts who then inhabited Britain and nearby parts of northern Europe.

Among other artifacts the excavators found on the hill was a long iron chain with several neck collars, a device researchers believe was used to control a gang of slaves. (In early America, such an artifact could have been used for either prisoners or slaves. But when the ancient Celts took prisoners, they almost always became slaves by default.) The researchers are able to connect the iron chain with Celtic slavery because of other evidence showing that in the era in question the local economy was based partly on slave labor. References to slavery appear in the writings of the ancient Greeks and Romans, who sometimes mentioned Celtic slaves used as commodities in trade. The first-century-B.C. Greek historian Diodorus Siculus, for instance, mentioned British Celts trading their own slaves in exchange for Roman wine and other luxury goods. Another piece of evidence is linguistic. The Celtic word for a female slave was synonymous with a unit of value used in economic transactions.

Exactly where the Celtic slaves came from is somewhat unclear. Most historians think the natives got them mainly through warfare (in which captives became slaves) or trade with Celtic societies on the nearby European continent.

The iron slave chains and collars from Bigbury Hill constitute an example of physical artifacts suggesting the existence of slavery in a given society or a specific historical period. More and more, modern scholars are able to combine such relics with other forms of evidence related to ancient slavery in Europe, Asia, Africa, and elsewhere in the world. Similar evidence has been found about slavery that occurred in later ages. It chronicles the exploitation of slaves in early modern times in the Caribbean islands, colonial America, the early United States, and other places. Using this growing trove of data, historians have managed to piece together a convincing case that slavery has existed in almost every human society throughout recorded history.

Understanding how and why some people enslaved others in the past is not a simple matter of intellectual curiosity. The fact is that slavery still exists today. Every single day of each succeeding year, human beings are held against their will in many countries, including the United States. When modern-day slavery occurs in countries such as the United States, it usually takes the form of human trafficking, in which vulnerable people, often the poor or immigrants, are controlled and exploited by more powerful people. Most people agree that this detestable and illegal practice should be eradicated. But if that were easy to do, it would have happened by now. Unfortunately, the criminals who deal in human trafficking are very skilled in evading law enforcement agencies.

## Evidence Informs Us

While members of law enforcement agencies and humanitarian organizations steadily work toward eliminating

*Although the Romans institutionalized slavery, they often freed slaves whose masters died.*

# The Celtic-Roman Slave Trade

The slave collars and chains found at Bigbury Hill in southern England are one of several kinds of evidence of a thriving ancient slave trade in the first century B.C. between the Romans and the Celts of Britain and other sectors of northern Europe. A Celtic slave was often traded for an amphora, or large storage container, of Italian wine. The slave then spent the rest of his or her life in a Roman city or on a Roman farm, as explained here by English scholar Stephen Allen.

> The [Celtic] seller would share the traded wine with his followers to enhance his status. As the demand grew for wine and other Mediterranean [luxury] goods, so did the need to find more slaves to barter. Celt and Roman soon came to depend on one another. . . . Some Celtic warriors found a kind of honorable death [as gladiators or animal fighters] in [Roman] arenas, but most ended their days in the [Italian] fields, toiling to produce the very wine they coveted so much.

Stephen Allen. *Celtic Warrior, 300 B.C.–A.D. 100: Weapons, Armor, Tactics.* Oxford: Osprey, 2001, p. 54.

slavery for good, archaeologists, historians, sociologists, and other scholars try to understand it better by studying its history. That endeavor relies almost solely on evidence. Why is concrete evidence so important in painting a clear picture of slavery? The answer is that numerous myths and false assumptions have existed, and still exist, about slavery.

For example, many people today assume that slavery has always been mainly about race, as it was when whites enslaved blacks in early America. The truth, however, is quite different. Throughout most of history, race played little or no part in the enslavement of human beings. Before modern times, the vast majority of slaves were war captives or people of low social status, and they represented all races.

Another common myth about slavery is that most slaves had only two ways to remedy their awful situation: attempt escape or commit suicide. In reality, fair numbers of slaves in the ancient world, especially in Greece and Rome, were freed by their masters. Indeed, some slaves actually bought their freedom using money they earned while enslaved.

Historians are able to separate such myths from the actual facts by diligently digging for tangible proof. As Columbia University scholar Richard C. Carrier explains:

Historians try to sort out the false or subjective [personal or one-sided] by employing the most proven means of distinguishing fact from opinion—evidence. [It] is naïve to suggest there is no truth in history to be sorted from the myths, falsities, and errors that seem the bread and butter of human thought. There are claims that are more probably true than others, many that are most probably true, and many more that are most probably false. And in every case, it is the evidence that informs us and puts a check on human opinion and ulterior motive. . . . True historians will identify every primary source, every shred of relevant evidence, so the reader will be able to check their claims. Where the evidence is incomplete and they have to speculate, they will admit it, keeping facts and judgment distinct.[1]

## Physical Evidence

Thus, archaeologists are gratified when they stumble on physical evidence of historical slavery such as the iron chains and collars from Bigbury Hill. Such artifacts are touchable and weighable—and most importantly, one can clearly see what they were used for. Besides iron chains and neck collars, physical evidence of slavery in past ages includes leg irons; slave bracelets and badges; houses, chambers, and barracks where slaves lived; ships that transported slaves; paintings and sculptures showing slaves and their masters; and various kinds of human remains, most often partial or full skeletons of slaves.

Among the partial bodily findings, teeth are particularly helpful to modern investigators. For example, excavators recently uncovered a cemetery in Campeche, Mexico, dating back to about 1550. The remains of 180 individuals were found and their teeth examined in a lab. The teeth in four of the bodies contained certain chemicals that show these individuals were not native to Mexico. Rather, they were born in western Africa. According to noted scholar John Noble Wilford, their teeth had

unusually high combinations of two isotopes of the element strontium. An isotope is a slight variation of a chemical element, with a different mass but otherwise the same as the basic element. . . . These strontium signatures enter the body through the food chain as nutrients pass from bedrock through soil and water to plants and animals. Different geologies yield different isotopic strontium ratios. This is locked permanently in tooth enamel from birth and infancy, an important tool to trace the migration of individuals. . . . In this case, the ratios of the isotopes strontium 87 and strontium 86 were consistent with those in the teeth and bones of people who were born and grew up in West Africa. A comparison with strontium measurements of people born in Mesoamerica [Central America] showed no similarities with the four specimens.[2]

Experts generally agree that this tangible evidence found in the four individuals' teeth shows they were Africans. Based on this discovery, experts make an educated guess that the individuals were slaves brought to the Americas to do manual labor. If this is true, these may have been the earliest African slaves ever to make it to the so-called New World. (The first African slaves in Britain's North American colonies—which would later become the United States—arrived in 1619.)

## Other Kinds of Evidence

Physical relics and remains are not the only kinds of evidence historians look at to learn about slavery in the past. For instance, numerous ancient and early modern societies left behind literary evidence for slaves and slavery. One of the earliest examples is *The Epic of Atrahasis*, from ancient Mesopotamia (what is now Iraq), where the Sumerian, Babylonian, and Assyrian civilizations flourished. The document dates from about 1650 B.C., more than thirty-six hundred years ago. But historians think the story told in it is many centuries older.

One of the most interesting things revealed in *The Epic of Atrahasis* is that the people of ancient Mesopotamia believed that slavery originated among the gods even before humans arrived on the scene. Indeed, the tale claims that humanity was initially created to perform slave labor, freeing some of the gods from that oppressive task:

> Great indeed was the drudgery of the gods, [because] the forced labor was heavy, [and] the misery too much. The seven great Anunna-gods were burdening the [lesser] Igigi-gods with forced labor. . . . The Igigi-gods were digging watercourses, canals they opened. . . . [They] dug the Tigris River and the Euphrates [River] thereafter. . . . They were complaining, denouncing, muttering down in the ditch: "Let us face up to our foreman . . . [so that] he must take off our heavy burden upon us! Enlil, counselor of the gods, the warrior, come, let us remove him from his dwelling!" . . . [Later they asked a goddess] "Will you be the birth goddess, creatress of mankind? Create a human being, that he bear the yoke . . . [and] let man assume the drudgery of the gods."[3]

Many other types of literary evidence for historical slavery exist. Among others, they include law codes from ancient Mesopotamia, ancient Rome, colonial America, and other past societies; passages in the Judeo-Christian Bible that mention slaves; treatises by ancient Greek philosophers and early modern thinkers discussing slavery's moral basis; descriptions of slaves in general and also of specific slaves by Roman writers; slave contracts from Rome, early modern America, and elsewhere; and

Roman documents granting individual slaves their freedom. An example of the latter comes from a last will and testament of a soldier named Antonius Silvanus, dating from A.D. 142. In drawing up the document, Silvanus made sure to address the matter of his personal slave's freedom: "As for my slave Cronio, after my death, if he has performed all his duties properly and has turned over everything to my heir above-named or to my trustee, then I desire him to be free, and I desire the five-percent manumission tax [a tax charged to owners who manumitted, or freed, their slaves] to be paid for him out of my estate."[4]

## Into the Realm of Emotion

To some degree, this Roman's concern for his slave's well-being goes beyond strictly weighable evidence. In a way, his words seem to transcend time and leap off the page into the realm of emotion, reminding us that both slave owners and their slaves have always been, first and foremost, human. Thus, tangible evidence can and ultimately *must* lead the investigator to explore the feelings of slaves and their masters.

A fine practitioner of that process is noted historian of ancient slavery Keith Bradley of the University of Notre Dame. He has been called an unusually thorough collector of hard evidence relating to his subject. Yet he has also managed to use such data to speculate about the thoughts, feelings, and suffer-

ing of slaves long dead. "What did it feel like to grow up as a slave," he asks,

perhaps to live well in a rich household, but gradually to come to realize that you were the symbol of everything that the powerful in society thought despicable, rotten and corrupt? What was it like to feel a sense of inferiority hammered into you every day by the food you were given to eat, the clothes you had to wear, the space you were supposed to sleep in? And what was it like to anticipate the lick of the lash, the clasp of the slave collar, the touch of the branding iron? To feel so desperate that you would run away and abandon all family ties and all the security of the household in an attempt to create a better life somewhere else, knowing that you would be hounded, perhaps recaptured and returned to a life more miserable than the one you had left?[5]

It is rarely possible to answer questions like these about the emotions of specific persons who have been dead for centuries. Yet good historians attempt to piece together educated guesses about such things. It is crucial to emphasize that these deductions are always based on as much physical, literary, and other tangible evidence as is humanly possible to gather. That relentless attempt to get at the truth lies at the very core of the historian's job.

# Chapter One

# Slavery in the Earliest Civilizations

The name, birthplace, and fate of the first slave is forever lost in the now murky events surrounding the rise of human cultures. Historians do think it is likely that slavery existed on a small scale in prehistoric times, the era before written records. They point to scattered evidence found here and there in northern Africa and the Middle East. For example, one of the leading historians of slavery, Hugh Thomas, writes, "Prehistoric graves in Lower Egypt suggest that a Libyan people of about 8000 B.C. enslaved a [weaker African] tribe. The Egyptians later made frequent [slave] raids on [villages] to the south and [later still] launched attacks by sea to steal slaves from what is now Somaliland."[6]

However, there is currently not enough solid evidence to reveal the exact point in prehistory that the institution of slavery emerged. For the moment, archaeologists and historians must use what they know about human economic and social history and habits to make some educated guesses. They suspect that slavery is a condition connected to settled, organized civilization—specifically agricultural societies with a stable food supply. Indeed, they say, it is unlikely there were any slaves in the long period before the development of agriculture, when people hunted and gathered their food. As historian Bamber Gascoigne explains it:

> Hunter-gatherers and primitive farmers have no use for a slave. They collect or grow just enough food for themselves. One more pair of hands is one more mouth [to feed and] there is no economic advantage in owning another human being. Once people gather in towns and cities, a surplus of food created in the countryside (often now on large estates) makes

possible a wide range of crafts in the town. On a large farm or in a workshop there is real benefit in a reliable source of cheap labor, costing no more than the minimum of food and lodging. These are the conditions for slavery.[7]

Whatever the conditions for the earliest slaves may have been, slavery became a fact of life for the first historic ancient civilizations, those that left behind written records. They include the peoples of Mesopotamia, Egypt, India, and China, among others. The four listed are often called the great "river civilizations" because they grew up on the banks of major rivers. They are also referred to as the "cradles of civilization" because they were the first large-scale, complex human societies. In addition, those cultures produced the earliest substantial evidence for slavery.

## Becoming a Slave in Mesopotamia

The first widely accomplished civilization that arose on Mesopotamia's fertile plains was that of the Sumerians. They took control of the region bordering the northwestern shores of the Persian Gulf around 4000 B.C. or somewhat later. Scholars are still unsure about their origins. They may have arisen from the area's earlier, less-advanced inhabitants; or they may have migrated into Mesopotamia from an unknown land lying further east.

Evidence shows that the Sumerians kept slaves. So did their immediate successors in the region—the Babylonians, who lived in southern Mesopotamia (at first called Sumer and later Babylonia); and the Assyrians, who dwelled in the north (initially called Akkad and later Assyria). However, slavery never became a large-scale institution among these peoples. Unlike what happened later in Rome and the early southern United States, the Mesopotamians did not rely heavily on slaves for most of the menial labor. Rather, the bulk of their public and private labor was performed by free people. Government-sponsored structures such as canals, temples, and palaces, for instance, were built mostly by farmers who worked on them part-time in the months between planting and harvesting. Therefore, most Sumerians, Babylonians, and Assyrians remained free. Slaves, who made up a small minority of the population, merely supplemented the workforce.

It appears that for a long time it was easy to differentiate between the unfree slaves and ordinary free citizens. This was because most slaves were foreign to some degree, from a cultural standpoint and probably in their speech and other ways as well. They were mainly war captives taken during raids into the lands situated beyond Mesopotamia's northern and western borders. This fact was reflected in the earliest Sumerian word for a slave. It translated as "man from the mountains." Other Mesopotamian slaves were born into slavery because their parents were slaves. Still others allowed themselves to become the temporary slave of someone to whom they

*This detail from an Assyrian relief sculpture depicts slaves at work. Although they had slaves, the Mesopotamians did not rely on them for menial labor. The bulk of public and private labor was performed by free people.*

owed money in order to pay back the debt, a practice known as debt bondage.

One reason that historians know these things is that Mesopotamian kings frequently bragged about their conquests in writings carved onto baked clay tablets or stone markers called stelae. A prominent example was the Akkadian king Rimush. His scribes described how in the late 2000s B.C. he raided Syria (lying along the Mediterranean coast to the west of Mesopotamia) and captured four thousand people. All of the prisoners were condemned to slavery.

## Work and Treatment

War captives like the ones King Rimush seized performed work falling into two broad categories. The first was laboring on state, or government-sponsored, building projects such as city defensive walls, palaces, ziggurats (large, pyramid-like religious structures), and canals. While working on such buildings, the slaves lived in makeshift huts erected near the work sites.

The other general kind of work done by Mesopotamian slaves consisted of domestic tasks performed in private homes. These included cleaning, cooking, looking after the family's children, and running errands. Not every home had slaves, mainly because poor people could not afford to house and feed them. But the average household likely employed from one to three slaves. Wealthy homes, in contrast, could afford to keep as many as forty or more slaves.

As in other slave-owning societies throughout history, the manner in which household slaves were treated in Sumeria, Babylonia, and Assyria varied from home to home. Some masters were strict and harsh and beat their slaves even for minor mistakes. Other slave owners were more humane and for the most part treated their slaves like part of the family. Still, even some of the kinder masters were not above selling a slave to another owner if the price was right, a situation that was no doubt upsetting, if not gut-wrenching, for the slave. Scholar Daniel C. Snell points out evidence that a female

## Debt Slavery in Babylonia

Debt slavery in Mesopotamian society was addressed in some of the law codes set down by Sumerian and Babylonian kings. King Hammurabi's list of laws, for instance, makes several mentions of the harsh custom of debt slavery. If a person owed a creditor a large sum of money and had no way to pay it back, he might sell himself, or his children, or even his entire family to the creditor. The debtor (or debtors) would continue to work as slaves for a set period as a substitute for the money owed. One of Hammurabi's laws named the terms and periods of enslavement involved in such an arrangement: "If any one fail to meet a claim for debt, and sell himself, his wife, his son, and daughter for money or give them away to forced labor, they shall work for three years in the house of the man who bought them, or the proprietor, and in the fourth year they shall be set free."

Ancient History Sourcebook. "Code of Hammurabi, c. 1780 BCE." Translated by L.W. King. Fordham University. www.fordham.edu/halsall/ancient/hamcode.asp.

slave named Usatusa found herself in that very situation. He reconstructed what her master may well have told her as she was about to leave for her new home: "You knew long ago that this day [might] come. And here it is. This is happening all over the place, people scaling back their staffs, and you shouldn't be surprised. . . . A deal is a deal. I [need] the money . . . and I'm going to carry it through now, no matter what you want."[8]

Some more positive family situations for Mesopotamian slaves did develop from time to time. In one, a master who had no children of his own legally adopted one or more of his most trusted slaves. This act was partly selfish, as it assured the slave owner that he would have someone to take care of him in his old age.

There were also cases in which a slave owner's wife was physically incapable of bearing children. If so, the master sometimes called upon a slave to have a child for him. Typically in such cases, the master legally adopted the child, who was not only a free person but also qualified to inherit part of the father's estate when the father died. One of the laws drawn up by the famous Babylonian monarch Hammurabi in the 1700s B.C. stated, "If his wife bear sons to a man, or his maid-servant have borne sons, and the father while still living says to the children whom his maid-servant has borne: 'My sons,' and he count them with the sons of his wife; if then the father die, then the sons of the wife and of the maid-servant shall divide the paternal property in common."[9]

Evidence also shows that some masters freed one or more of their slaves for various reasons of their own. Those freed slaves, appropriately called "freedmen," got paying jobs, and some became successful businessmen. This indicates that slavery was not always a hopeless condition in Mesopotamian society.

## Egyptian Slaves

Not far to the west of the ancient Mesopotamian plains lay another great river civilization—Egypt, land of kings called pharaohs and the famous pyramids in which some of the pharaohs were interred following their deaths. Like the Sumerians, Babylonians, and other peoples of Mesopotamia, the Egyptians had slaves. However, modern experts frequently find it difficult to differentiate between slaves and free workers in ancient Egypt. This is because unfree ancient Egyptian individuals did not fit the most common definition for slaves in most of history's slave-owning societies.

For example, in many slave-owning societies slaves had no legal rights, could not own property, were not allowed to marry free people, and according to law or custom, they could be abused and even killed by their masters. This was not the case in Egypt. Although Egyptian slaves could be bought, sold, and owned, they had certain fundamental rights. They could earn money, own property, and marry anyone they desired, including free people if both parties wanted it that way.

However, one should not interpret these facts to mean that all Egyptian

*An Egyptian scribe is depicted registering Nubian slaves in this relief sculpture. Although Egyptian slaves could be bought, sold, and owned, they had certain rights: They could earn money, own property, and marry anyone they desired, including a free person, if both parties consented.*

slaves had it easy or were well treated. Evidence shows that there could be many downsides to their lives. Most Egyptian slaves were war prisoners or convicts, and the rest were poor peasants or children born of slaves. Like slaves in all times and places, they were expected to do their masters' bidding, no matter how difficult or humiliating the job might be.

A majority of Egypt's slaves worked on large agricultural estates operated by noblemen or temple priests. Some of the others toiled in mines, digging for copper and other metals. Contrary to many mistaken modern depictions in movies and elsewhere, Egypt's great pyramids were not erected by slaves. Rather, those structures were built by free agricultural peasants who did the work when they were not planting or harvesting their crops.

Egypt also had household slaves, as other historical slave-owning societies did. It appears that these unfree servants were treated more humanely than other Egyptian slaves and in a number of cases were able to gain their freedom. In stark contrast, the slaves who labored in mines led miserable and relatively short lives and rarely, if ever, obtained freedom. The second-century-B.C. Greek geographer Agatharchides, who lived for a while in Egypt, described the plight of these unfortunate souls, saying in part, "The worst of fates falls to those whom the . . . government sends off to the bitter slavery of the . . . [gold] mines, some to suffer along with their wives and children. They are a sad sight, their clothes girded up and just enough to cover their private parts. . . . All who suffer [this] fate . . . feel that death is more desirable than life."[10]

## Slavery Along the Indus and Ganges

The incidence of slaves toiling in mines was not unique to Egypt. The ancient civilization that grew up along the Indus and Ganges Rivers in India also employed slaves for such purposes. However, as in Egypt, most Indian slaves worked as domestic servants in peoples' homes. Indeed, most middle- and upper-class Indian families had slaves.

These families got their slaves in a variety of ways. Some were prisoners captured in wars fought among Indian states. Others were non-Indians purchased in other countries by Indian traders, who then sold them to Indian customers. Still others were children born to slaves who were already part of a family. Debt bondage, which occurred in neighboring Mesopotamia, was also fairly common in ancient India, and the Indians had laws dealing with persons who sold themselves into slavery to help pay their debts. For example, a law said that if a temporary debt slave committed a crime while in that position, he or she automatically became a slave for life.

Like slaves throughout history, ancient Indian slaves sometimes had to perform difficult or unsavory jobs. However, their lives were not necessarily insufferable or hopeless. Evidence suggests that quite a few domestic Indian slaves were mostly tasked with doing the household cleaning, cooking, gardening, and child rearing. Moreover, the law limited the severity of punishments a master could impose on his slaves.

Also, some laws even imposed fines on overly unreasonable, greedy, or brutal masters. According to an ancient Indian treatise, *The Arthashastra*, a law stated, "Deceiving a slave of his money or depriving him of the privileges he can exercise [by law] shall be punished with [a] fine." Indian law also frowned on a fairly common practice among slave owners through the ages—sexually abusing their slaves. "When a man commits or helps another to commit rape with a girl or a female slave pledged to him," one law said, "he shall not only forfeit the purchase-value, but also pay a certain amount of money to her and a fine . . . to the government."[11]

The money a slave should not be deceived of in the first law consisted of income he or she was allowed to earn while enslaved. With the master's consent, a slave could work outside the home, receive payment for it, and spend the money any way he or she wanted. In addition, the slave could save up money and purchase his or her freedom, assuming the master approved. Some masters also let their female slaves marry free men and live in their husbands' houses,

# The Toil of Mine Slaves

The ancient Greek geographer Agatharchides described what life was like for the Egyptian slaves who worked in the country's gold mines in the second century B.C.

The rock of the mountains in which the gold is found is sheer and very hard. [The slaves] burn wood fires and render it spongy with heat, and then go at working it, cutting the parts softened up with quarrying tools. . . . Those who are young and strong quarry the gleaming stone with iron picks, delivering their blows not with any particular skill but just force. . . . They do their quarrying with [small oil] lamps bound to their foreheads. . . . Constantly shifting the position of their bodies, they knock down chunks—not according to their bodily condition and strength, but to the foreman's eye, who never fails to administer punishment with the whip. Young boys, creeping through the galleries hacked out by the miners, laboriously collect what has fallen down on the gallery floor and carry it outside the entrance. . . . Now starts the work of the women. [A] large number of grinding mills are placed in a row, and the pounded rock is put in them. The women . . . grind away . . . until they have reduced what is measured out to them to the consistency of fine flour.

Quoted in Karl Müller. *Geographi Graeci Minores*. Hildesheim, Germany: Olms, 1990, pp. 124–127.

*Slaves labor in a Greek mine on this depiction based on a painting of a sixth-century-B.C. Corinthian vase.*

as long as the slaves returned to their masters' houses each day to do certain chores.

## Buried Alive in China

At least at first, slaves led much more precarious and often shorter lives in China, the great river civilization lying directly north of India. Slavery in China existed for at least eighteen hundred years. The first written evidence for the institution appeared in the Xia Dynasty (family line of rulers), which lasted from about 2070 to 1600 B.C.

Slaves under the Xia and their immediate successors in China were mostly

*Chinese slaves labor on the Great Wall. Chinese slaves were treated harshly and, in the end, mercilessly. Many of them are buried in the wall they helped build.*

enemy soldiers taken in battle, captured criminals, or extremely poor folk who could barely support themselves. For the most part they performed the most difficult agricultural work. Also, some slaves worked in the homes of the well-to-do. As might be expected, the emperor could afford to own more slaves than anyone else, so imperial slaves numbered in the thousands. Over time in China, a handful of the most talented and trusted imperial slaves were allowed to work in important positions on government projects like tax collecting and erecting public buildings.

Whatever they did for work, initially all Chinese slaves were treated strictly, harshly, and in the end mercilessly. After a master died, his slaves were killed or buried alive. Either way, they accompanied him in death so that they could continue serving him in the afterlife. Luckily for China's slaves, over time various leaders called for abolishing this brutal practice and placing pottery representations of slaves in masters' tombs instead. Nevertheless, some well-to-do Chinese continued taking their slaves with them in death.

In the more enlightened Tang Dynasty (A.D. 618–907), slaves were mostly criminals and foreigners. Among those foreigners were people given as tribute (gifts given by one party to acknowledge submission to another party) to Chinese emperors by the leaders of subject peoples. As one modern expert explains, such human gifts included

> skilled artists and entertainers. The king of Tokhara, a nation north of

modern Afghanistan and Pakistan, sent a painter of extraordinary skill to the Chinese court. . . . He was best known for his Buddhist icons, but also executed works depicting flowers and birds. The most celebrated of the slaves, however, were troupes of musicians, singers, and dancers who performed at court banquets and other functions.[12]

## Other Early Slave Societies

Among the world's oldest societies, the big river civilizations usually left behind more in the way of written records and other forms of evidence than others. In the cases of most ancient cultures, however, very little is known about slavery and the lives of slaves. This is certainly true of the Etruscan city-states that grew up in northwestern Italy in the early first millennium B.C. (One reason historians see Etruscan history and culture as crucial is that the nearby Romans borrowed numerous customs and ideas from the Etruscans, who were for a long time more culturally advanced.)

Of the few facts known about Etruscan slaves, one is that there were a lot of them compared to the numbers of free people. Also, Etruscan slaves did all the hard, tedious, and/or distasteful tasks. Among these were quarrying, street cleaning, agricultural labor, and mining.

A bit more is known about Etruscan freedmen, former slaves who had been freed by their masters. These freedmen frequently worked as shopkeepers, artisans, farm overseers, secretaries, and other professional positions that the Etruscan nobles felt were beneath their dignity. A freedman usually maintained close ties to his former master, a custom that passed on to the Romans.

Slavery also existed to the south of Italy, in ancient Africa, where black people regularly enslaved other blacks. Most details about how the institution worked in the earliest times remain unclear. Some ancient African peoples seem to have viewed slaves merely as chattel, or property. As a rule, they acquired slaves to do heavy labor, to serve a master's sexual desires, or to increase a master's social status. However, other African peoples viewed slaves as less worthy individuals who could be trained and redeemed enough to become part of the family and community. In fact, a few ancient African groups permitted slaves to rise to fairly high ranks in local armies.

Evidence is also sparse for slavery in the early civilizations of Mesoamerica, including the Aztec civilization, which was later conquered by the Spanish in the early modern era. Aztec slaves were called *tlacotin*. As in all ancient societies, a large proportion of them were either war captives or criminals who were enslaved as a punishment. Interestingly, debt bondage, which existed in ancient Asia and Europe, developed independently among the Aztecs. One thing that was markedly different about Aztec slavery, however, was that it was not viewed as hereditary. That is, children born of a slave were free people, not slaves.

Thus, although some scattered facts about slavery in early history have survived, it is not yet possible to piece together a single comprehensive picture of the institution during those long centuries. The earliest slave owners were not "concerned to write works about slavery or individual slaves," Keith Bradley points out. Such sources would have allowed modern observers "to have a direct view of the institution's material conditions."[13] The first such comprehensive sources about slavery were compiled by the ancient Greeks, so their society is the next logical one to examine in the long, painful story of human slavery.

# Chapter Two

# Slavery Defined as Natural: Ancient Greece

The Greeks were the first known ancient people to develop a slavery institution big enough to support or drive a major portion of their economy. Slavery never became as large-scale and complex in Greece as it eventually did in Rome. Yet a majority of the Greeks' menial work was performed by slaves, and nearly every Greek either owned one or more slaves or interacted with slaves on a fairly regular basis. In fact, in Athens, from which most evidence for Greek slavery comes, slaves were so numerous and well integrated into society that it was often hard to tell who was a slave and who was not. According to an anonymous fifth-century-B.C. Athenian, "You can't hit [the slaves] there [in Athens], and a slave will not stand aside for you [when you meet him in the street]. . . . If it were customary for a slave . . . to be struck by one who is free, you would often hit an Athenian citizen by mistake on the assumption that he was a slave. For the people there are no better dressed than slaves."[14]

## As a Rule, Decently Treated

The fact that most Athenian slaves looked no different than their masters was not the only reason people did not usually strike slaves in the street. Another reason was that a majority of slaves were well behaved enough that masters rarely felt compelled to strike them. In turn, slaves were so often well behaved because, with some marked exceptions, they were well treated.

Most slaves in Athens, and presumably the bulk of other Greek city-states, fell into four groups. Private (or domestic) slaves worked as servants in private homes; commercial slaves were clerks or laborers in local shops; public slaves were assistants to various town officials; and agricultural slaves did farmwork. Obedient household slaves tended to receive lenient treatment in part because they frequently became trusted members of the family. Another reason they and most members of the other slave groups were generally well treated was that they were viewed as valuable property. The common wisdom was that a master could not best reap the benefits of owning a slave if that slave was physically injured or emotionally distressed.

*A Greek funerary monument shows a slave holding a baby while her mistress looks on. In general, Greek slaves were decently treated and often became part of the family.*

In fact, maintaining the financial value of slaves was so important that it came to be supported by law. In Athens, a free individual who abused or killed another person's slave could be prosecuted in court. Also, it was illegal for an owner to take the life of his own slave, no matter what the slave's offense. Evidence for this takes the form of a speech penned by the Athenian orator Antiphon in about 419 B.C. Even slaves who slay their masters, he states,

are not [permitted to be] put to death by the relatives of the deceased. The relatives hand them over to the authorities, in accordance with [Athens's] laws. The law allows a slave to give evidence against a free man in a murder charge, and allows a master, if he so desires, to prosecute anyone who kills his slave. The law has equal force against a man who kills a slave and against him who kills a free man.[15]

## Exceptions to the Rule

Every rule has a few exceptions, and such was the case with the treatment of Greek slaves. There was a second class of public slaves in Athens made up of laborers who sweated day in and day out in the city-state's silver mines. These workers were shackled with chains at all times, forced to work under terrible conditions, and had no hope of gaining their freedom. It appears that slaves perceived to be dangerous, unruly, or unworthy in some way ended up in the mines. Moreover, it was not unusual for a master whose private slave was repeatedly disobedient to send that slave to the mines for a few weeks. The intent was to show the slave how well off he was in his master's home and scare him into shaping up.

Another slavery group with members who were poorly treated as a matter of course existed in Sparta, in southern Greece. Sparta was a very atypical Greek state in a number of ways. One way the Spartans were different than the norm was that they enslaved other Greeks, which was generally frowned on among the city-states. Most slaves in Greece were non-Greeks who were captured in wars or bought from slave traders, although smaller numbers were bred in the home.

The Spartans first broke this unwritten cultural rule in the 600s B.C. To the disdain of most other Greeks, they conquered the neighboring city-state of Messenia and enslaved all of its inhabitants. No other Greeks dared to try to help the Messenians, because Sparta had the most feared army in Greece. (This situation endured until 371 B.C., when Thebes decisively defeated Sparta, forever ending the myth of Spartan invincibility. After that, the Messenians regained their freedom.)

The Spartan slaves, who came to be called helots, were treated harshly and at times cruelly. The noted first-century-A.D. Greek writer Plutarch described one of the many ways that Spartans humiliated helots. "They would force them . . . to drink quantities of unmixed wine [the Greeks normally diluted their wine with water] and then would bring them into the mess halls to show the young men what drunkenness was like. They would also order them to perform songs and dances which were vulgar and ludicrous."[16] Also, the helots had no legal protections like those from which Athenian slaves benefited. Spartan citizens regularly beat and sometimes killed helots at will and with no fear of prosecution.

## Jobs of Domestic Slaves

Not much is known about the numbers of slaves in Sparta and how they were assigned to do various jobs either for the state or individual citizens or families. But modern historians have reached a consensus that in Athens and other more mainstream states, a home of average means probably had two or three slaves. In comparison, a well-to-do family likely had fifteen to twenty slaves.

Of those domestic slaves, women formed a higher proportion than men, partly because household tasks were widely seen as "women's work." For example, female household slaves helped the master's wife do the spinning, weaving, cooking, and cleaning. They also nursed her babies and aided her in raising the family's children.

Some Greek slave women were seen as capable and trustworthy enough to manage an entire household for their owners. This appears to have happened often in cases in which a well-to-do man owned a country home that needed to be maintained when he and his family were living in town. In a treatise on the proper running of a country estate, the Athenian historian Xenophon described a fictional but typical Greek upper-class landowner named Ischomachus (probably modeled on Xenophon himself). Ischomachus and his wife hired a new housekeeper for the estate and observed that she was very

self-disciplined with regard to food, drink, sleep, and sex, and who, in addition, struck us as having the best memory and being most likely to avoid incurring our disfavor by neglecting her duties. . . . We taught her to be prepared to work hard for the increase [success] of our estate. . . . We also instilled justice [honesty] in her, by rewarding right, not wrong, among the servants and by showing her that justice leads to a wealthier and freer life than injustice.[17]

Xenophon's treatise on country estates also provides evidence for another common duty of female Greek slaves—to have sexual relations with the master. Ischomachus states that when his young wife is wearing makeup and dressed nicely "she becomes an object of desire, and especially because she is granting her favors willingly." By contrast, he declares, "the servant has no choice but to submit."[18] (In the modern world, such sexual exploitation is viewed as a serious form of abuse. In Greece, Rome, and most other ancient lands, however, it was widely seen as natural and acceptable.)

# Hunting the Spartan Helots

The helots significantly outnumbered native Spartan citizens, who regularly worried that the slaves might rebel. Indeed, fear of rebellion was part of the Spartan rationale for the harsh and at times inhuman treatment the helots endured. In addition to backbreaking work from sunup to sundown and beatings for the slightest infraction, they were subject to state-supported murder committed by young men in military training. The first-century-A.D. Greek biographer Plutarch wrote: "Periodically, the overseers of the young men would dispatch them into the countryside . . . equipped with daggers and basic rations, but nothing else. . . . At night, they made their way to roads and murdered any helot whom they caught. Frequently, too, they made their way through the fields, killing the helots who stood out for their physique and strength."

Plutarch. "Life of Lycurgus." In *Plutarch on Sparta*, translated by Richard J.A. Talbert. New York: Penguin, 1988, pp. 40–41.

While female household slaves usually outnumbered the male ones, the latter performed a number of essential jobs. They did the shopping, or at least helped the master do it; made repairs to the house and property; took the master's son to school and monitored his behavior there; and accompanied and saw to the safety of the women of the house when they appeared in public. Male domestic slaves also carried messages, ran errands, and on occasion (if there was a national emergency) fought alongside their masters in battle.

## Slaves Outside the Home

Whatever their sex, household slaves were considerably fewer in number than those who worked in shops, for the state, and in the fields. For example, evidence indicates that the Athenian orator and writer Lysias and his brother, who ran a shield-making shop, employed more than one hundred slaves. Most of these workers probably had originally been trained by Lysias's father, Cephalus, who had started the business.

Public slaves were also numerous and held important, productive jobs in Athens and other Greek states. According to the late French scholar Robert Flacelière, many of these unfree workers were clerks and

other underlings who served the [government], the law courts, or the offices of the various civil authorities—indispensable cogs in the administrative machine and the nearest we get, in Athens, to any sort of permanent civil service. There were also such state employees as the public executioner . . . the street sweepers, the skilled workers in the mint who struck Athens's [coins], and [a group of archers] responsible for policing the streets, the Agora [marketplace], [and] the law courts.[19]

In his work the *Athenian Constitution*, the famous fourth-century-B.C. Athenian scholar and thinker Aristotle provided specifics about some of the jobs of the slaves who worked for what Flaceliere called the "civil authorities;" that is, Athens's elected government administrators. "They [the slaves] keep watch to prevent any scavengers from depositing [manure and other refuse] within a mile and a quarter of the [town] wall. And

*A Greek inscription from the sixth century B.C. lists the names of public slaves and their jobs. Public slaves held important, productive positions in Athens and other Greek city-states.*

# Slaves in Greek Markets

One of the more important jobs performed by ancient Athenian slaves was overseeing weights and measures in the city's public marketplace. An inscription found by archaeologists tells what the work involved and how slaves who tried to take advantage of their positions were punished. "They must provide equivalents of the weights and measures [i.e., show that their weights follow official standards] to the government officials and to all other persons who ask for them . . . and they must not carry anything out of the buildings provided, except for the lead or copper equivalents. But if they [attempt to carry away silver] . . . [the officials] are to punish the slave[s] . . . by whipping."

Quoted in Thomas Wiedemann, ed. *Greek and Roman Slavery*. Baltimore: Johns Hopkins University Press, 1981, p. 157.

*Athenian slaves oversaw the weights and measures used in trading in the Agora, Athens's marketplace.*

they prevent the construction of buildings encroaching on and balconies overhanging the roads. And they remove for burial the bodies of persons who die on the roads."[20]

Those Greek slaves who worked on farms performed jobs no less crucial to society than commercial and public slaves did. Like their counterparts in Mesopotamia and Egypt had done before them, agricultural slaves in Greece planted, harvested, and threshed grain; pruned vines; and tended to sheep, goats, pigs, and other livestock. If their master was a practicing farmer, these slaves quite often worked side by side with him and members of his family. (In contrast, some farm owners were absentee landlords who lived in the towns and left the actual farmwork to their slaves.)

It is important to note that in Athens, Thebes, Corinth, and most other places in Greece, slaves played only a supporting role in agriculture. The reason was that these city-states, which viewed themselves as independent nations, were dominated by free peasant farmers who worked their own lands, usually with only minimal help. A major exception was Sparta during the period that it enslaved the Messenians. In those years the oppressed helots were forced to do all of the agricultural tasks, which totally freed male Spartan citizens to pursue political, military, and other endeavors. Despite the fact that his own city-state opposed Sparta in most things, Aristotle felt that the highly repressive Spartan agricultural approach was worthwhile. In his *Politics*, he promoted the idea that Athens should adopt that approach, saying,

> The people who cultivate the land should be slaves. They should not all come from the same tribe or nation, and they should not be too courageous. This will make them useful workers and safe from the danger of revolt. As a second best [approach], they should be non-Greek-speaking serfs with natural characters as similar as possible to those I have indicated. Those of them who are used on private estates must be private property, and those used on community land public property.[21]

## Slavery a Natural Condition?

Some people today express surprise and a little disappointment to hear a person of Aristotle's obviously high intellect talk about enslaved fellow humans with such contempt and lack of sympathy. But once again, one must consider the time in which he lived. He and his fellow Greeks, as other ancient peoples did, accepted the existence of slavery as a perfectly natural condition. Indeed, they were convinced that the gods fully endorsed the institution.

This is why Aristotle, Plato, and other profound thinkers advocated ways to improve society and the human condition on the one hand, and on the other could not imagine a society operating efficiently without slave labor. Aristotle defined a slave as "a human being who by nature does not belong to himself but to another person," as well as a piece of property. He added that any person who becomes a slave to someone else "is by nature a slave (for that is why he belongs to someone else). . . . Nature must therefore have intended to make the bodies of free men and of slaves different also. Slaves' bodies [are] strong for the services they have to do, [whereas] those of free men [are] upright and not much use for that kind of work, but instead useful for community [i.e., political] life."[22]

Another way that the Greeks, along with some other ancient peoples, saw slaves as humans who were mentally and morally deficient, dishonest, or otherwise naturally substandard. Because they were dishonest by nature, the thinking went, they could not be trusted and therefore had to be fairly regularly supervised or watched. Xenophon's country gentleman Ischomachus says

*The Greek philosophers Plato and Aristotle, depicted here in an ancient Greek relief, accepted the existence of slavery as a perfectly natural condition approved by the gods.*

# The Richest Freedman in Athens

Noted historian and University of Louisville professor Robert. B. Kebric here briefly summarizes the highlights of the life of Paison, the most successful freed slave in Athenian history.

> He was born about 430 B.C. and while his name is Greek, his background was probably Phoenician. He was purchased by two Athenian bankers [and] near the end of the fifth century [B.C.] he began working for them. Because of his good character and honesty, Paison earned his owners' respect and, eventually, was freed and assumed responsibility for the business. By 394/393 B.C., he apparently owned the bank, probably first leasing, then purchasing it from his former masters. . . . In the years that followed, Paison gave the city a thousand shields, produced in his own shield factory. . . . Such generosity did not go unnoticed, and for his efforts, which included other [gifts to the state], he was awarded Athenian citizenship. [This] allowed Paison to own property. By the time of his death, he had real estate, including his house in the Piraeus [Athens's port town] and blocks of apartments he rented.

Robert B. Kebric. *Greek People*. New York: McGraw-Hill, 2005, p. 220.

that a master or his overseer "must be capable of supervising and scrutinizing the [slave's] work, must be prepared to show gratitude for work performed well, and must not be afraid of administering punishment when irresponsibility demands it."[23]

Evidence that the vast majority of Greeks agreed with this view of slaves as morally deficient can be seen in the comedies penned by the Athenian playwrights of the fifth and fourth centuries B.C. The slaves portrayed in these works were almost always devious, shifty, lazy, cowardly, sex-crazed, or some combination of these negative traits. (They were also frequently depicted as witty and clever, which shows that the Greeks grudgingly recognized that slaves could possess good traits, too.)

What the slaves themselves thought about the way free people viewed and portrayed them may never be known. This is because no slaves left behind writings telling how they felt about this and other important social issues. One might suppose that Greek slaves thought they were just as good as free people and that slavery was immoral or otherwise wrong. But this was almost certainly not the case. Like their masters, slaves thought slavery was natural and inevitable. This is shown by the fact that many of the slaves who were able to gain their freedom immediately acquired slaves of their own.

## Becoming a Freedman

The number or proportion of Greek slaves who managed to get manumitted, or acquire freedom and the title of freedman, is unknown. But the number of manumission contracts that have survived suggests that the practice was fairly common. True, a master could free a slave merely through a verbal declaration in front of a reliable witness. However, this was difficult to prove if someone disputed it later, when the former master was either dead or mentally incapacitated. So it became customary to draw up a formal document announcing that an owner was awarding freedom to his slave. One of these contracts reads in part, "On the following conditions, Sophrona [the owner], acting with the consent of her son Sosandros, hands over . . . to be free the female house-born slave named Onasiphoron."[24]

The motives of Greek masters for freeing slaves were many and varied. Evidence indicates that one of the more frequent reasons was to offer a slave a gesture of thanks for many years of loyal, effective service. Also, at least in some cases, money was a major incentive.

*An ancient Greek inscription details the manumission of slaves. As freedmen, former slaves could now make many more decisions about their own lives.*

When in need of ready cash, some slave owners viewed their slave's offer to buy his or her freedom for a lump sum as a smart financial move. As for where this money came from, many domestic slaves received periodic small wages, more accurately described as tips, for hard work and/or good behavior. They could spend the money at their leisure. Or they could save it up over time with the long-range goal of buying their freedom.

From the point of view of some Greek slaves—namely those who did not like their owners—manumission had one big disadvantage. In whatever way they had attained freedom, there was rarely a clean break with the former master. By tradition, and sometimes by legal agreement, the freedman was obligated to work for his or her previous owner for a certain number of years. Often it was the rest of the former master's life, as was written into Onasiphoron's manumission contract: "Onasiphoron is to remain with Sophrona for the whole period of the latter's life, doing whatever she is ordered to do without giving cause or complaint. If she does not do so, then Sophrona is to have the power to punish her in whatever way she wishes. And Onasiphoron is to give Sosandros a child [have a baby with him]."[25] This evidence demonstrates that in many cases a freedman was still tightly bound to the previous owner despite being technically free.

Such burdensome obligations aside, becoming a freedman had a major advantage. This was that the former slave could make many life decisions on his own and strive to better himself and become a more important and hopefully admired member of the community. If while a slave he had worked as a laborer in a shop, for example, upon gaining freedom he could become a part or full owner of the business and share in its profits.

Furthermore, a freedman could become as financially successful as circumstances allowed. The most prominent example of such success was that of an Athenian freedman named Paison. When he passed away in 370 B.C., he was the wealthiest banker and manufacturer in Athens and left his eldest son a valuable estate.

Success stories like Paison's were very unusual. Most slaves in ancient Greek society never achieved freedom. Moreover, the situation for Greek slaves did not improve over time. For the remainder of antiquity (ancient times), slavery was an accepted institution in Greece, and no one made any serious attempt to abolish it. If that institution did nothing else, it set an example for the Romans, who eventually conquered the Greek-controlled lands of the eastern Mediterranean region. The Greeks had shown that a society-wide slave system could work and be profitable. In their turn, the Romans applied the same idea on a scale greater than anyone had ever seen or would ever see again.

# Chapter Three

# Slavery on an Immense Scale: Ancient Rome

L ike the Mesopotamians, Greeks, and others before them, the ancient Romans kept slaves. Also like the Greeks, the Romans accepted slavery as a natural and inevitable part of the human condition. In an attempt to use this belief as a justification for their slavery institution, the Romans, who were widely known for their complex legal system, carefully explained the difference between slaves and free people in their laws. Two of their many statutes relating to slavery were:

Slavery is an institution of the common law of peoples by which a person is put into the ownership of somebody else, contrary to the natural order. . . .

The principal distinction made by the law of persons is this, that human beings are either free men or slaves. Next, some free men are free-born, others freedmen. The free-born are those who were free when they were born; freedmen are those who have been released from a state of slavery.[26]

The Romans felt compelled to both define and justify slavery mainly because slaves played so many varied and important roles in their society. In fact, Rome had more slaves and relied more heavily on slave labor than any other nation or empire in world history. Along with their renowned army, slavery was one of the Romans' two biggest and most multifaceted institutions. Slaves, freedmen, and the social customs and laws pertaining to them permeated Roman life at all levels—including the family home and/or farm; markets and commercial enterprises; shipping, construction, manufacturing, and other industries; painting, sculpture, music, and other arts; and the law courts and government services.

*Roman slaves wait to be sold in the marketplace. Slavery became institutionalized in Roman life at all levels of society and government.*

Because of the sheer size and complexity of slavery in Roman society, it encompassed many different beliefs, concepts, feelings, traditions, and other driving forces, or dynamics. But the strongest dynamic of all, overriding all the others, was the total domination of powerless people by powerful ones. In Keith Bradley's words:

The power that lay at the disposal of the Roman slave owner was the power of life and death, and slavery itself was viewed in many ways as a state of living death. . . . The victor in battle had the right to kill the vanquished. If however, the victor spared the vanquished and enslaved him instead, the latter continued to live, but only in a condition of suspended death [that could be altered at any time by] the owner. The slave's very identity, in fact, now depended on his owner. This was the source of the slave owner's power.[27]

## Sources of Slaves

It is important to emphasize that slavery was not practiced on an immense scale throughout Roman history. The ancient Roman civilization existed for more than twelve centuries (roughly 753 B.C. to A.D. 476), during which it first went from a small city-state ruled by kings to a rapidly expanding republic governed by representatives of the people. Finally, in its last five centuries, it became a giant empire lorded over by a succession of emperors.

The number and importance of slaves in Roman society varied widely over the course of that national evolution. The period in which Rome had the most slaves and was most dependent on them spanned the four centuries that began in about 200 B.C. and ended in about A.D. 200. That fateful era roughly covered the last two centuries of the Roman Republic and first two centuries of the Roman Empire. The reason that Roman slavery expanded so much in the last years of the

*Captives who will become slaves are marched before the public in a Roman triumphal parade. Rome conquered many lands beyond Italy, and huge numbers of war captives flooded into the Roman heartland as slaves.*

# How Did It Feel to Be a Slave?

In writing about Roman slavery, a noted expert on the subject, Keith Bradley, points out that there are many questions about Roman slaves that people today cannot answer. Yet merely posing and pondering these questions, he says, "is to go a little way towards defining the psychological climate under which Roman slaves lived and to understanding the pressures that had to be balanced against one another for the sake of human survival." Among these questions, Bradley says, are:

> what [was] it like to be a captive of the Roman army and to know . . . that the only future you faced was to be butchered or sold off into servitude?… What did you feel when your wife and children were torn away and handed over to slave-dealers . . . to be sold on the [auction] block and never seen again? What was it like to feel powerless when the woman you called your wife was stripped naked and mercilessly flogged by the master in full view of the household?… Or what did it feel like to grow up as a slave [and] gradually to come to realize that you were the symbol of everything that the powerful in society thought despicable, rotten, and corrupt?

Keith Bradley. *Slavery and Society at Rome*. New York: Cambridge University Press, 1994, pp. 179–180.

Republic, researcher Matthew Bunson points out,

> was Rome's rise as the most powerful state in the Mediterranean [world]. With territorial acquisitions in Asia Minor [what is now Turkey], many of the slaves came from the East, and were Syrian, Jew, Greek, and even Egyptian. Further conquests along the Rhine [River, in what is now Germany], the Danube [River, in what is now Austria], and in Gaul [what is now France] opened up even more services for strong [foreigners] who made good fieldhands.[28]

Thus, before this period of expansion, when Roman lands were still confined mainly to the Italian Peninsula, nearly all Roman slaves were of Italian birth. Over time, however, as Rome's conquests added lands beyond Italy, huge numbers of war captives flooded into the Roman heartland as slaves. In the late third century B.C., for instance, the Romans acquired many thousands of prisoners in the Second Punic War (fought against the nation of Carthage, centered in North Africa). Almost all of them became slaves. By the end of that conflict, in 201 B.C., Roman society was in a sense addicted to slaves, which were employed to fill a growing labor vacuum created by increasing numbers of free men entering the military.

As time went on, the slave ranks grew apace. At least 150,000 Germanic tribesmen were captured and enslaved in 101 B.C. alone, and close to half a million residents of Gaul were enslaved by Roman general and statesman Julius Caesar when he conquered that area in the 50s B.C. Incredibly, by the close of the Republic in the late first century B.C., slaves made up fully one-third of Italy's overall population of 6 to 7 million!

During these same centuries, conquest was increasingly supplemented by piracy as a major source of Roman slaves. Typically, pirates would capture unwary travelers and then sell them in slave markets. "For almost a century from about 167 B.C.," the late historian P.A. Brunt wrote, "piracy flourished in the eastern Mediterranean. The Romans long took no effective action against it, [partly] because their slave owners were indirectly the beneficiaries. The free port of Delos [in Greece] could handle 10,000 [slaves] a day, and the pirates must have been the main suppliers."[29]

## Domestic Slaves and Their Duties

As in other historical slave societies, that of Rome also came to acquire slaves through domestic slave breeding. By the time slave breeding had become a major source of slaves, the large population of private slaves was a fact of life in towns across the Roman realm. The number of slaves in an average household was between two and ten, depending on a family's means. Upper-class Romans owned many more slaves, of course— from a few dozen to several hundred. The richest Romans had thousands. Evidence shows that a freedman named C. Caelius Isidorus, who managed to amass a fortune after the noted writer Pliny the Elder freed him, owned 4,116 slaves. But as excessive as this sounds, it did not compare to the slave-keeping facilities of the Roman emperors. On average, each of them owned up to 20,000 slaves!

Whoever owned them, slaves fell into two principal categories—private slaves, in Latin *servi privati*, and public slaves, or *servi publici*. With some exceptions, private slaves usually had easier jobs and enjoyed better treatment than public ones. Moreover, of a master's private slaves, the ones who had been born and raised in his home were often seen as part of the family and therefore enjoyed comforts and privileges that a majority of slaves did not. One scholar remarks, "Normal masters could hardly fail, even if half-ashamedly, to have a soft spot for characters they had seen toddling and growing up about the place."[30]

Still, even those slaves bred in the home suffered the indignity and personal limitations that automatically came with being unfree. They had little or no control over their own lives and fate, and they had to obey the master no matter what he ordered them to do. If they disobeyed him, they could expect some sort of punishment, even if he was normally a kind individual. In most situations, therefore, domestic slaves did what they were told and performed their duties without complaint.

In smaller households, those duties were fairly few and standard—cleaning, cooking, gardening, helping with the spinning and weaving, running errands, and watching over the family children. By contrast, in larger households that had dozens of slaves or more, their duties were more numerous and varied. Some wealthy homes had slaves who worked as midwives, bakers, food tasters, barbers, and financial managers. The largest and richest household of all, that of the emperor, featured all of these plus many slaves with even more specialized skills, including architects, painters, cupbearers, silversmiths and goldsmiths, actors, and musicians, among many others.

## Other Kinds of Slaves

Another kind of private slave belonged to a group known as *familia rustica*, meaning "farm slaves." During the four centuries in which slavery was at its height in the Roman realm, most members of this group worked on large farming estates. In general, their lives were physically more difficult than those of household slaves, and many of the tasks farm slaves performed were menial and sometimes monotonous.

The highest-ranking and most responsible position for agricultural slaves was the job of *vilicus*, or estate manager, for a wealthy absentee landlord. The manager oversaw all the other farm slaves and made sure the estate ran smoothly. Lucius Junius Columella, a first-century-A.D. Roman estate owner who wrote a book about proper farm management, listed the traits that best qualified a slave for the job of *vilicus*. Especially important, Columella said, was the man's age:

> He should no longer be a young man, since this will detract from his authority to command, since old men don't like to obey some youngster. Nor should he have reached old age yet, or he will not have the stamina for work of the most strenuous kind. He should be middle-aged and fit and know about agriculture, or at least be so dedicated that he will be able to learn quickly.[31]

One of the slaves the manager had charge of was his female companion. She not only did typically women's duties like spinning, weaving, and cooking, but also acted as a nurse for the other slaves when they were sick or injured. Other farm slaves planted and harvested crops, took care of the farm animals, dressed grape vines and collected the grapes to make wine, dug irrigation and drainage ditches, and cleaned stables.

A third branch of private slaves were those who served as assistants, apprentices, or laborers for masters who owned or ran businesses. As was the case in Greece, they (and other kinds of private

*The lives of Roman farm slaves were physically more difficult than those of household slaves.*

slaves) sometimes purchased or were given their freedom. Upon becoming freedmen, most continued to work in the same commercial profession they had before. The difference was that as freedmen they had the option of owning a business of their own.

Some public slaves also had socially prominent jobs requiring skill and a strong sense of responsibility. Most public slaves worked for the central government, individual towns, or the emperor. A majority of freeborn Romans, particularly those in the upper classes, viewed not only menial labor but also jobs like tradesman, craftsman, business manager, and government administrator as beneath their dignity. So most members of the staffs of governors and emperors were slaves or freedmen. In

this way, a number of public slaves came to wield more influence than many of the freeborn Romans who considered them social inferiors.

Other public slaves worked in diverse occupations, some of them skilled and some not, and some of them backbreaking and dangerous and some not. These jobs were in areas such as mining, quarrying, and road building; cleaning and maintaining aqueducts, sewers, and city streets; tax collecting; assisting priests in temples; overseeing public markets; maintaining state mints, libraries, treasuries, and financial accounts; and fighting as gladiators in amphitheaters like the famous Colosseum. Put simply, public slaves kept the proverbial wheels and gears of the Roman state turning.

# All Men Are Slaves

Not every Roman held slaves in contempt. The first-century-A.D. philosopher and playwright Seneca felt that slaves were simply fellow humans who had fallen on hard times and deserved humane treatment. In a letter to his friend, Lucilius, governor of Sicily, he said:

> I am glad to learn . . . that you live on friendly terms with your slaves. This befits a sensible and well-educated man like yourself. "They are slaves," people declare. Nay, rather they are men. "Slaves!" No, comrades. "Slaves!" No, they are unpretentious friends. "Slaves!" No, they are our fellow-slaves, if one reflects that Fortune has equal rights over slaves and free men alike. . . . They are not enemies when we acquire them. We make them enemies. . . . He whom you call your slave sprang from the same stock . . . and [like you and me] breathes, lives, and dies. . . . This is the kernel of my advice: Treat your inferiors as you would be treated by your betters. . . . "He is a slave." His soul, however, may be that of a free man. . . . Show me a man who is not a slave; one is a slave to lust, another to greed, another to ambition, and all men are slaves to fear.

Seneca. "Epistle 47." In *Moral Epistles*, vol. 1, translated by Richard M. Gummere. Cambridge, MA: Harvard University Press, 1961, pp. 301–303, 307, 311.

*The first-century-A.D. Roman philosopher Seneca believed that slaves were fellow humans who had fallen on hard times and thus deserved humane treatment.*

# The Slave Rebellions

All of this shows how thoroughly slavery saturated Roman society and made a majority of free Romans dependent on their slaves. Because Roman masters were in a very real sense surrounded by slaves, society was marked by an almost constant undercurrent of fear that the slaves might suddenly turn on their masters. Indeed, the sheer numbers of slaves made their banding together and going on a killing spree a very real and frightening prospect. To help ensure that this did not happen, during the late Republic and early Empire, masters usually did not allow their slaves to have ready access to weapons. Slaves were also prohibited from serving in the army, where they would receive both weapons and combat training.

These fears of slave insurrections and the safety measures designed to prevent them were neither paranoid nor overreactions. Three major slave rebellions rocked the Roman realm within a period of only about seventy years. The first two occurred in Sicily, the large island off Italy's southwestern coast, from around 139 to 132 B.C. and from 104 to 100 B.C. Both uprisings were quickly crushed.

The third slave revolt—led by the now famous Spartacus—took place in Italy from 73 to 71 B.C. A war captive, Spartacus had been enslaved and assigned to a gladiator school in Capua, about 100 miles (161km) south of Rome. While still in training, he managed to escape, along with several other slave-gladiators. As Plutarch told it, the slaves "had done nothing wrong, but, simply because of the cruelty of their owner, were kept in close confinement until the time came for them to engage in combat. Two hundred of them planned to escape, but their plan was betrayed and only seventy-eight . . . [acted] in time and [got] away, armed with [meat] choppers and [roasting] spits which they seized from some cookhouse."[32]

In the days and weeks that followed, the escapees, with Spartacus as their leader, began to free slaves and steal weapons from towns and farms across the nearby countryside. The leaders of the movement trained many of the liberated slaves to fight. This proved effective, as the growing slave army defeated one after another of the small Roman armies sent against it. Eventually, Spartacus commanded forces exceeding seventy thousand in number.

Jolted into action by a wave of fear spreading through Italy, the central government finally allocated the resources necessary to stop Spartacus. Marcus Licinius Crassus, a rich financier who was trying to build a major political reputation, wrangled command of a large contingent of battle-hardened troops. In a furious battle fought in Lucania in southern Italy, the slaves put up a truly heroic defense. But it was in vain. They went down to defeat for the simple, stark reason that no slave army was big enough or well-trained enough to stand up to the full-blown Roman military establishment,

*Spartacus's rebellion was crushed by Marcus Licinius Crassus in Lucania in 71 B.C.; nevertheless, it was one of history's more daring slave revolts.*

which had conquered much of the known world. The memory of Spartacus's defeat made this clear to the slaves of succeeding generations, and Rome saw no more slave rebellions.

## Discipline and Punishments

Just as Roman masters quite often feared their slaves, many slaves had good reason to fear their masters. Some of those owners treated their slaves in a generally humane way, as a majority of Greek slave owners did. However, plenty of evidence reveals that there was a darker, more sadistic side of Roman

masters' treatment of slaves. Although out-and-out brutal masters who openly abused their unfree servants appear to have been in the minority, they nonetheless existed in every generation. In their households, chaining, starving, severe whippings, branding with hot irons, breaking the ankles, and even castration were employed as punishments.

Furthermore, even the most liberal and humane slave owners routinely exploited and disciplined their slaves. In such homes, taking away privileges, boxing the ears, and mild flogging with ropes or whips were the most frequent forms of discipline. Both female and male slaves were sexually exploited on a fairly routine basis as well. At the time, this was not intended or seen as a punishment. Yet at the least, it was one more of many factors that constantly reminded the slaves of their fundamental inequality and indignity in Roman society. It is no wonder that a certain level of fear and tension always percolated just beneath the surface of slaves' everyday lives.

This unwholesome apprehension felt by many slaves, especially when compounded by the beatings or other violence of a brutal master, sometimes prompted a slave to run away. Unfortu-nately for him or her, an escaped slave, called a *fugitivus*, was almost always easily caught. The fact was that few people, including most fellow slaves, were likely to help a runaway in a society in which slavery was widely viewed as natural and acceptable. Indeed, most people saw the escapee as a thief who had stolen his master's property—specifically himself.

Moreover, slave owners frequently offered rewards for capturing and returning *fugitivi*. Archaeologists have found reward notices in Egypt from the centuries when that land was ruled by Rome. One reads, "A boy named Hermon has run away. [He is] about 15, wearing a

*Even the most liberal and humane slave owners routinely exploited and disciplined their slaves. In such homes, taking away privileges, boxing the ears, and mild flogging with ropes or whips were the most frequent forms of discipline.*

cloak and a belt. Anyone who brings him back will receive . . . 3 talents [then a large sum of money]. Anyone who gives information that he is at a shrine [seeking refuge will get] 2 talents."[33]

Slave masters also had the option of hiring detectives who specialized in catching escaped slaves. Still another reason the slave was likely to be recaptured was that most Roman slaves who ran away more than once or twice were branded and/or collared. The usual practice was to burn the letter F (for *fugitivus*) onto the slave's forehead. In addition, the metal collars slaves wore around their necks commonly featured inscriptions that identified the owner. An example found by modern excavators says, "I have escaped. Arrest me [and] take me back to my master Zoninus and you will be rewarded with a gold piece."[34] It was also fairly routine more simply to etch the letters *T.M.Q.F.* on a collar. They stood for *Tene me quia fugio*, meaning "Arrest me since I am a fugitive."[35]

Needless to say, the punishments meted out to slaves who ran away were often harsh. They might be beaten mercilessly or have an arm, a leg, or both permanently crippled. Repeat offenders were sometimes sent to the mines or to the arena to face gladiators or animals, both of which meant certain death. People who made the mistake of helping escaped slaves were also guilty of a crime. One law stated, "Anyone who has hidden a runaway slave is guilty of theft [and] any person whatsoever who apprehends a runaway slave has an obligation to produce him in public."[36]

Such laws eventually became meaningless because the immense slavery institution that helped make Rome successful during the period of its political and military height ultimately died out. Roman slavery was not abolished. Indeed, even the Christians, who took charge of the Roman state in the fourth century A.D., made no serious attempt to get rid of slavery. Rather, as an examination of medieval European society indicates, after Rome fell, its former lands underwent a profound economic transformation that basically made chattel slavery unnecessary.

# Chapter Four

# The Early Modern Slave Trade Develops

Ancient Rome and Greece, with their large-scale slavery systems, faded into oblivion in the fifth and sixth centuries A.D., marking the end of antiquity and the start of Europe's medieval era. The small, scattered societies that grew upon Rome's mighty wreckage had no major slavery institutions of their own. So for a period of close to eight hundred years, chattel slavery—the outright ownership of one person by another—was virtually unheard-of in Europe.

The reason for this transformation was not abolition, since the Romans had never made any attempt to ban slavery. What happened instead was the onset of an economic change in which the cheap labor of serfs substituted for the cheap labor of slaves. Medieval serfs were free people who were so poor that they came to depend on and largely did the bidding of a few wealthy landowners. In a nutshell, because of the availability and easy exploitation of serfs, medieval Europeans had no particular need for slaves.

The situation began to change in the 1400s and 1500s. In those years a growing number of European and Middle Eastern explorers, traders, and national leaders began to find and exploit new lands and economic markets beyond their familiar territories. These lands were primarily in Africa, North and South America, and East Asia. The peoples of these lands were generally less technically and militarily advanced than the exploiters. So the latter realized it would be both easy and profitable to enslave portions of the native populations. In this way a new and in time large-scale slave trade developed, one that was in some ways reminiscent of, but in other ways even more brutal than, the Roman version.

## From Slavery to Serfdom

Although serfs largely replaced Roman slaves in early medieval Europe, their

*Roman* coloni, *poor tenement farmers, were bound by their unfortunate circumstances—and often legally, too—to serve their wealthy landlords virtually for life.*

serfdom was based directly on Roman models. Throughout the years of the Roman Empire (30 B.C.–A.D. 476), large agricultural estates could be found across Rome's European territories. At first, most of the laborers on those estates were slaves. However, between about 300 and 450, Rome's economy steadily worsened. Roman coins progressively declined in value, taxes rose sharply, large numbers of people fell into debt, and poverty spread and deepened.

The upshot of these disastrous economic trends was that many formerly middle-class Romans sank into the lower classes. Among them were small farmers who, though never rich, had at least owned their land and homes. As time went on, increasing numbers of them had to abandon their farms. Some moved to big cities to search for steady work or get free food handouts from the government. An even larger number of the former small farmers offered their services to the owners of the big farming estates.

These destitute folk now became what the Romans called *coloni*. The term meant poor farmworkers who were bound by their unfortunate circumstances—and often legally, too—to serve their wealthy landlords essentially for life. One way of looking at the plight of these so-called slaves of the soil was that a *colonus* was technically a free person. Yet he was so poor and dependent on his lord that realistically he had nowhere else to go but the estate of another rich landowner. The late historian Michael Grant explained that the *coloni* were not true slaves, but rather foreshadowed

the serfdom of the Middle Ages. Some of these men may already have been deeply in debt to the landowner before they arrived on his estate. From that time onwards . . . they had to [give the owner] a huge proportion of the crops they were allowed to produce on his land, or sometimes served directly as part of his labor force. In return, they hoped to be able to rely on their new landlords to chase the government's tax collectors away.[37]

The wealthy landlords who employed these quasi-serfs were extremely successful, so much so that they survived Rome's political collapse. They went on to become some of the earliest medieval lords, with their manor houses, extensive fields and orchards, and large numbers of serfs to maintain them. It made no sense to enslave these workers. After all, if the landowners did that, they would have to feed and clothe them, whereas free serfs were expected to feed and clothe themselves. Hence, serfdom made more economic sense in that situation.

## The Trans-Saharan Slave Network

As long as that particular situation remained the norm, the need for slaves remained nearly nonexistent in medieval Europe. However, outside of Europe during this period, slavery was still alive and well. Several of the societies that flourished along Europe's borders, especially those of the Arabs and other Muslims in the Middle East and North Africa, maintained small but profitable traditional slavery systems.

Most of the slaves exploited in these lands were obtained from sub-Saharan Africa. This came about in part because Islamic law states that Muslims cannot enslave one other. To find slaves, therefore, Muslim merchants and slave catchers had to go to foreign lands, and they were pleased to find a plentiful source of black Africans dwelling not far south of the vast Sahara Desert's arid reaches.

After capturing a group of Africans, the traders sold them to home and farm owners in the Middle East and North Africa, where many of the newly enslaved individuals toiled as field hands, domestics, and mine laborers. Other black slaves were coerced into converting to Islam and served in Muslim armies. There, over time, because of their intelligence and courage, they were entrusted with a great deal of responsibility and military authority. Bamber Gascoigne points out one surprising outcome of this trend:

The Muslim habit of using slaves in the army . . . led to one unusual result, in itself an indication of the trust accorded to slaves in Middle Eastern communities [in those centuries]. In 1250 the slave leaders of the Egyptian army, known as Mamelukes, [overthrew] the sultan and [seized] power. A succession of rulers from their own ranks [ruled] much of the Middle East, as the Mameluke dynasty, for nearly three centuries.[38]

Whether the displaced Africans were soldiers, farmworkers, or mine laborers, according to modern scholars an estimated 10 million of them became slaves in Muslim lands from the 600s through the 1700s. This trans-Saharan slave network was never as large as the transatlantic (or Atlantic) slave trade that followed it. Yet the Muslim version served as a model for the later system.

## Enter the Genoese and Portuguese

In fact, the European-controlled transatlantic slave trade began as an effort to compete with the Muslim slave network operating south and southeast of Europe. In the 1300s the Genoese (the residents of the Italian kingdom of Genoa) began to develop an interest in operating sugar plantations. They saw that the sugar plantations run by Muslims in Egypt, Syria, and other areas of the Middle East were extremely lucrative. It made sense, therefore, to copy the Arab model, which included capturing and enslaving black Africans. Throughout the fifteenth century, Genoese plantation owners purchased Africans through the trans-Saharan network. They put these slaves to work on plantations set up on Cyprus and other Mediterranean islands.

Just as the Muslim versions had been, the Genoese plantations proved to be reliable moneymakers. So it is not surprising that other Europeans were eager to get

## African Nations Devastated by the Slave Trade

When the Portuguese began negotiating with the leaders of African nations for slaves, they maintained good relations with those nations. But over time the growing European thirst for slaves seriously damaged several African peoples, as explained by historian S.I. Martin.

> The Kongo [or Congo] was devastated by its relationship with Portugal. First contact was in 1482 and initially the Kongolese were hopeful that it might be a beneficial relationship based on equality, and there was even an exchange of Ambassadors and the Royal family were baptized into the Catholic Church. However over the next few decades the interest shifted towards the slave trade. The [Kongolese] king at this time, Alfonso I, despite his efforts to ban the trade, lost half of his kingdom to slavery. In 1611 even the Portuguese king was so concerned at the impact slavery was having, he tried to ban whites from the interior, but this [order] was later rescinded.

S.I. Martin. "Slavery in Africa." Anti-slavery International. http://old.antislavery.org/breakingthesilence/slave_routes/slave_routes_portugal.shtml.

*Slaves are marched to work in Africa by armed guards.*

involved. The first were the Portuguese, who set up large sugar plantations on the Cape Verde Islands, Madeira Islands, and Canary Islands (all situated off Africa's northwestern coast) in the 1440s and 1450s. At first, the owners used mostly white European workers. They included orphans, condemned prisoners, and indentured servants (free persons who agreed to work for a specified period in exchange for transportation, food, or some other necessity). In time, however, such workers became harder to find.

So the Portuguese turned to enslaving sub-Saharan Africans. Their ship captains explored Africa's western coast and negotiated with local chieftains for slaves. This proved profitable for both parties at first. But in time the growing trade in slaves proved damaging for a number of African societies, as explained by researcher S.I. Martin:

The Portuguese explored and claimed more of the West African coast and islands, with trade being established with Ghana, Benin, Gabon, and Mali in quick succession in the 1470s. The Portuguese established treaties with some nations, often trading weapons for slaves. This had repercussions, leading to warfare, starvation and ultimately depopulation in some [African] regions. . . . Bases were established [by the Portuguese] on small islands off the West Coast of Africa, the most important being Cape Verde and Sao Thome. These were used for collecting slaves traded from the mainland, who were then sent to Lisbon [Portugal's capital]. The development of sugar cultivation on Sao Thome provided the blueprint for the [later] larger plantation economy of the Americas.[39]

# Initial American Slave Societies

The next step in the ongoing development of the Atlantic slave trade occurred in the 1500s with the creation of new European plantations in the Americas. Like those on several European islands, these came to use the forced labor of captured black African slaves. The owners of the American plantations directly copied the successful São Thomé sugar-producing operation. The first American version was established on the Spanish-held island of Hispaniola, located east of Cuba, in 1502. The Spanish sank a great deal of money and other resources into these ventures in hopes of outdoing the Portuguese and other Europeans who had operated such plantations before them.

At first, the Spanish tried to use local Native Americans rather than Africans on their New World plantations. The intent was to save the extra cost of importing slaves from faraway Africa. This approach proved disastrous, however. The native slave laborers rapidly died out or became too few in number to turn a profit. On Hispaniola, for instance, out of lack of foresight and sheer cruelty, Spanish landowners and their over-

seers acted against their own interests by working to death or simply murdering the natives, while large numbers died from infectious diseases brought to the island by the newcomers. By 1515, 80 percent of the island's original 250,000 inhabitants had perished, and by 1650 all of the local natives were gone.

To replace those they had eradicated, the Spanish began importing black Africans. According to scholar Johannes Postma, "Africans became the preferred labor force," of the Spanish American colonies. More and more, the Spanish and other Europeans tended to refrain from enslaving their fellow whites and to exploit black Africans instead. Only "people who were different," particularly racially so, says Postma, "were made chattel slaves. In that sense, Europeans acted like Muslims, who enslaved outsiders, or 'infidels,' but protected fellow Muslims from that fate."[40]

This racially motivated exploitation of Africans was readily adopted by other Europeans in the Americas, including the Portuguese in Brazil beginning in 1538, the English in Barbados starting in 1627, and the French in the Caribbean colony of Saint Domingue from the 1600s on. By the late 1700s the tremendously profitable Saint Domingue colony had a staggering 455,000 black slaves.

Looking back at these developments from today's more enlightened times, the capture and enslavement of so many individuals from a different race appears unbelievably ignorant and cruel. However, the Europeans who perpetrated these crimes against humanity actually thought they were merely taking advantage of

# Equiano's Overland Journey

Former slave Olaudah Equiano educated himself and in 1789 penned a book describing his experiences as a slave. In this passage, he tells how, after he and his sister were captured in their village, they were taken across western Africa to the Atlantic coast.

[We] came at length to a country the inhabitants of which differed from us in [numerous] particulars. [They] ate without washing their hands. They cooked also in iron pots and had European cutlasses and crossbows, which were unknown to us. . . . At last I came to the banks of a large river, which was covered with canoes in which the people appeared to live with their household utensils. . . . I was put into one of these canoes and we began to paddle and move along the river. . . . Thus I continued to travel, sometimes by land, sometimes by water, through different countries and various nations, till at the end of six or seven months after I had been kidnapped I arrived at the seacoast.

Olaudah Equiano. *Equiano's Travels.* Edited by Paul Edwards. Oxford: Heinemann, 1996, pp. 13–14.

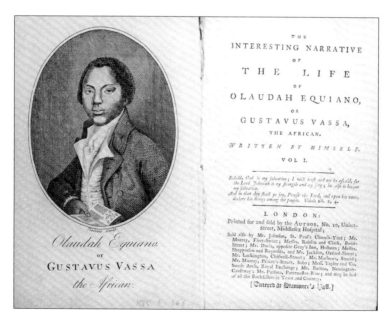

*Former slave Olaudah Equiano published his book on his life as a slave in 1789.*

a system designed by God for the ultimate benefit of the white race. Nonwhite native peoples possessed a lesser form of intelligence, the thinking went. From the 1600s on, whites who enslaved blacks fell back on a rationale, or justification, that was eventually expressed in writing by a French nobleman. "The negroid [black] variety [of human] is the lowest [of the races], and stands at the foot of the ladder," he arrogantly stated.

> The animal shape that appears in the shape of the pelvis is stamped on the negro from birth, and foreshadows his destiny. His intellect will always move within a very narrow circle. . . . White peoples [in contrast] are gifted with . . . an energetic intelligence. . . . At the same time, they have . . . an extreme love of liberty. . . . [History] shows us that all civilizations derive from the white race, that none can exist without its help and that a society is great and brilliant only so far as it preserves the blood of the noble group that created it.[41]

## The Dreaded Middle Passage

This distorted kind of thinking became a central underlying pretext for using black Africans as slaves throughout the Americas, including the region that would later become the United States. In order to support the American colonies that used those slaves, the Atlantic slave trade expanded and became brutally efficient. The exact size and scope of the trade, which reached its height in the 1700s, is uncertain. But the general consensus of most scholars is that between 10 million and 12 million slaves crossed the Atlantic Ocean against their will over the course of roughly three centuries. They also estimate that as many as a third of them died during the voyage.

The slaves perished during the dreaded middle passage, as the trip came to be called, because of a combination of factors. These included overcrowding, horrendously unsanitary conditions, extreme cruelty on the part of the slave dealers, and the psychological distress of the captives. People today know about these horrors thanks partly to descriptions penned by a few white witnesses. There are also a handful of eyewitness accounts by Africans who actually suffered through the ordeal and later became educated and wrote about it.

The fullest surviving African account is that of Olaudah Equiano, who was taken from his village in eastern Africa as a young man in the mid-eighteenth century. He later recalled the conditions aboard the slave ship, describing the stench that pervaded the boat's below-deck holds. It was there that hundreds of slaves lay or sat shackled, sweating, vomiting, and/or bleeding from numerous untreated wounds and skin sores. Equiano wrote:

> I received such an [odor] in my nostrils as I had never experienced in my life. So that with the loathsomeness [nastiness] of the stench and [people] crying together, I became so sick and low that I was not able

to eat. [The guards punished me for refusing to eat.] One of them held me fast by the hands and laid me across . . . the windlass and tied my feet while the other flogged me severely. I had never experienced anything of this kind before.[42]

Another account of the horrible conditions aboard the slave ships was provided by an English doctor named Alexander Falconbridge. Writing in 1788, he said that the slaves were forced to lie on their backs and were often packed into spaces measuring only 18 inches (46cm) in height, so that they could barely maneuver enough to change positions. They were also chained by the neck and legs,

he reported. "In such a place," he wrote, "the sense of misery and suffocation is so great that" the slaves were "driven to frenzy."[43] Meanwhile, the bodies of the poor wretches who died on the ships were routinely thrown overboard.

## The Triangular Trade

The North and South American colonies that used the survivors of the middle passage for their plantations developed a very profitable commercial network that spanned the entire Atlantic region. It was known as the triangular trade because it featured three primary legs, or profit-producing steps. The first leg consisted of the export of goods from Europe to Africa. European merchants

*Sale of African slaves to southern U.S. plantations was the second "side" of the Atlantic slave-trade triangle. The other two sides comprised the selling of European goods to African leaders for slaves and the selling of products produced by slave labor to European markets.*

# A Horrendous and Traumatic Event

The transatlantic (or Atlantic) slave trade was an enormous and inhumane centuries-long practice that impacts the history of hundreds of millions of people alive today. Indeed, the directors of an African American group that regularly calls attention to the slave trade calls it "probably the most horrendous and traumatic event [ever to occur] in the Western hemisphere." They add:

> To the descendants of Africans now residing in North America, South America, and the Caribbean, it is definitely the most significant event in our history. . . . [It] turned portions of the African continent into chaos, empires rising and falling based on their quota of slaves. The brutalities and degradation these victims existed under was daily and never-ending. And the legacy would continue to their children and descendants for generations to come. This was . . . an event which destroyed peoples and whole cultures; an event which would destabilize a continent, changing it forever; an event which would enrich Europe, create empires, and [help] build America.

Assata Shakur Forums. "The Maafa: A Holocaust of Greed," July 13, 2005. www.assatashakur.org/forum/post-translated/9002-maafa-enslavement-africans-timeline.html.

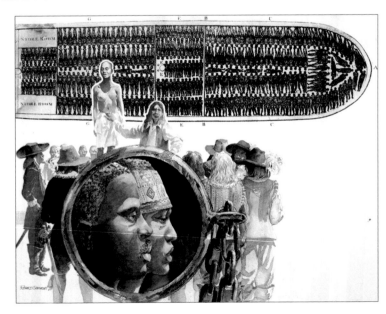

*The era of the transatlantic slave trade is seen by many today as the most horrendous and traumatic event in Western history.*

struck deals with African chieftains who owned large numbers of slaves and traded these goods—including liquor, fabrics, and gunpowder—for slaves.

The second part of the Atlantic triangular trade consisted of the sale of the slaves in the Americas. First, the slave traders turned a tidy profit. Second, the buyers—the plantation owners—benefited because the slaves they purchased were inexpensive to feed and clothe. The slaves were also cheap enough to make it viable to regularly replace agricultural slaves who died from overwork.

The third and final leg of the triangular trade consisted of the sale of goods produced by the slaves in American colonies to markets in Europe. Sugar, cotton, tobacco, molasses, rum, spices, and other goods turned out by American plantations and farms flowed into Europe, turning still another profit for enterprising traders. With this profit, merchants bought the necessary trade goods to use in Africa, in the first leg of the next three-way trading cycle.

## Abolition at Last

Luckily for the slaves, who were the chief commodity involved in the triangular trade, not everyone was content to see other human beings treated so badly. During much of the eighteenth century, a movement intent on ending the Atlantic slave trade gained steam. Abolitionists existed throughout Europe and in other countries around the globe, but they were most numerous in Britain and the United States. The spirit of these crusaders for justice was ably captured by the case of an English slave trader who became a prominent abolitionist. That extraordinary individual, John Newton, later wrote about his remarkable conversion. "During the time that I was engaged in the slave trade," he said, "I never had the least scruple as to its lawlessness." He added,

> I was, on the whole, satisfied with it, [thinking of it] as the appointment Providence [God] had marked out for me. . . . I only thought myself bound to treat the slaves under my care with gentleness. [But I eventually saw that what I was doing was wrong.] I consider myself bound in conscience to bear my testimony at least and to wash my hands from the guilt [and] to take shame to myself by a public confession, which, however sincere, comes too late to prevent or repair the misery and mischief to which I have formerly been accessory.[44]

Thanks in part to Newton and other righteous and courageous individuals like him, in 1807 the British became the first people in the world to ban the slave trade. In that same year, legislators in the United States, urged on by President Thomas Jefferson, passed a law abolishing the trade (though not slavery itself). It actually went into effect on January 1, 1808.

The British were also instrumental in getting other nations to abolish the slave trade. Initially, British leaders primarily employed diplomacy to accomplish this

# Black Slaves in Latin America

In addition to the many Africans who ended up as slaves in North America and the Caribbean islands, even more were forced into slavery in Central and South America. Life for black slaves in some of these areas was horrendous, and the death rate for slaves on the sugar plantations in Brazil and elsewhere in South and Central America, sometimes called Latin America, was high.

The customs of slavery in the largely Spanish/Portuguese regions differed in a number of ways from those of slavery in the American South. According to Kjartan Sveinsson, senior research and policy analyst for the Runnymede Trust, Spanish slave owners were guided, to a greater or lesser extent, by a centuries-old statutory code known as the *Siete Partidas*, which viewed slavery as a necessary evil but also provided slaves some rights and protections under the principle that "any slave (including Africans) were potential Christians and thereby servants of the king. The extent to which these principles translated into practice are debated, but it appears that the dehumanisation of African slaves was less pronounced in Spanish America than in French and British colonies." Historians frequently note, for example, that slaves in the Spanish and Portuguese colonies often intermarried with nonslaves, including the Europeans and the native peoples of the countries. Also, some slaves in Latin America were taught to read and write, and many were instructed in the Catholic religion. The lives of slaves varied greatly throughout Latin American regions, however, and slaves working in mines or in sugar plantations experienced truly brutal conditions.

Many Latin American nations abolished slavery when they gained independence from Spain. This was decades before the United States got rid of slavery in the 1860s. One notable exception was Brazil, which did not ban slavery until 1888.

Kjartan Sveinsson. "Slavery in Latin America." Real Histories Directory. www.realhistories.org.uk/articles/archive/slavery-in-latin-america.html.

aim. At an international meeting held in 1815 in Vienna, Austria, for example, British pressure helped push the French and Dutch into eradicating the trade. Two years later the Spanish and Portuguese also bent toward the British position by agreeing to keep their slave ships restricted to the sea lanes south of the equator and well away from most of Britain's colonies.

Not long after that, however, Britain became more aggressive in its efforts to end the now steadily shrinking African slave trade. In 1819 a group of British warships started patrolling the Atlantic. The captains of these vessels searched for and either captured or sank slave ships from numerous countries. Soon the French and Americans joined in this endeavor, and slave dealers now found themselves hunted as international pirates and criminals. More than one hundred thousand African slaves were rescued and freed by the British, French, and Americans during these years.

Abolition of the African slave trade was a major, triumphant moment in the long, misery-causing history of human slavery. However, it was only the kidnapping, enslavement, and overseas shipping of Africans that ended. Slavery itself was still a fact of life in a number of countries, where slave owners simply replaced the importation of slaves from afar with local breeding efforts. The injustice and brutality of the remaining slave systems is well illustrated by a brief look at slavery in the pre–Civil War United States.

# Chapter Five

# That "Peculiar Institution": Slavery in America

As ancient Rome had, the southern sector of the early United States practiced slavery on a large scale. The country had been founded and initially settled largely by people from the British Isles, and it was mainly English slave traders who had brought the first African slaves to colonial America in the 1600s and early 1700s. Between 1720 and 1730 alone, those traders had transported more than ten thousand slaves from western Africa to the colonies of Virginia, Maryland, South Carolina, and Georgia.

The biggest increases in unfree African workers in the colonies occurred in Virginia and Maryland. Surviving Virginia census records show that in 1671 the colony had about two thousand blacks, who made up around 5 percent of the overall population of forty thousand. By 1700, only twenty-nine years later, Virginia had sixteen thousand transplanted Africans, accounting for

more than 30 percent of the population. Maryland witnessed similar dramatic increases in its black slave population during the same period.

Such increases continued throughout the colonial American South, and by the mid-1700s a large part of British America was economically dependent on the forced labor of Africans. Shortly before the American Revolution (in the 1770s), the thirteen British colonies were home to more than three hundred thousand slaves, who constituted at least one-fifth of the population. Almost every person in the southern colonies either used black workers, *was* one of those workers, or used products or services provided by such workers.

When the colonies broke away from Britain and established the United States, Virginia's Thomas Jefferson urged the other founding fathers to abolish slavery—despite the fact that he owned slaves himself.[45] But the slavery institution was then so deeply entrenched in the South that Jefferson and those who agreed with him were outvoted. Even after Britain and the United States banned the slave trade in 1807, that "peculiar institution," as southerners later came to call it, remained in force. It took decades of concerted efforts by the abolitionists and a bloody civil war to finally rid the country of a practice that had long made a mockery of Jefferson's immortal words, "All men are created equal."[46]

## Fellow Sufferers?

During the early colonial period, the large-scale planters who saw a pressing need for increasing amounts of cheap labor did not at first turn to importing Africans for this purpose. The initial plan was to exploit the labor of the local Native Americans. Quite soon, however, it became clear that the Indians were going to be too hard to enslave. They were "tough, resourceful, defiant, and at home in the woods, as the transplanted Englishmen were not,"[47] historian Howard Zinn pointed out.

It did not take long, therefore, for the American planters to follow the lead of the Spanish and Portuguese in the Americas and begin importing black African slaves. These Africans were no less tough than the American Indians, but certain factors made them easier to exploit as slaves. Most notable was the fact that the Europeans had attempted to enslave Indians in lands that the Indians' ancestors had occupied for countless generations. The Indians knew the American region well; they had familiar places they might escape to and could sometimes seek help from native groups in surrounding areas. In contrast, the captured blacks had been ripped from their native lands and cultures, taken thousands of miles away, and thrown into a strange land. If they managed to escape, there were no familiar places or friendly neighbors to support them. The chances of survival alone in the harsh and unknown environment were grim. This was the case for the first twenty Africans in colonial America when they arrived in Jamestown, Virginia, in 1619. Nearly every year thereafter, more black slaves came to the colonies and found themselves in the same basically hopeless situation.

For a while, however, the custom was to supplement the black slave laborers with white indentured servants. The latter had voluntarily signed contracts. In exchange for their passage to America, they promised to work for the planters for a certain number of years. Between 1620 and 1660, these servants worked right alongside the black slaves. Indeed, during an average work week, both white and black workers put in the same number of hours. Moreover, evidence from Virginia indicates that early black and white laborers shared the same bunkhouses, ate the same foods, and on occasion had children together. The Africans, who were still fairly few in number, were seen by poor whites more as fellow sufferers than as inferiors. As a result, overt racism based on skin color was not yet a significant factor in the social situation of black slaves in America.

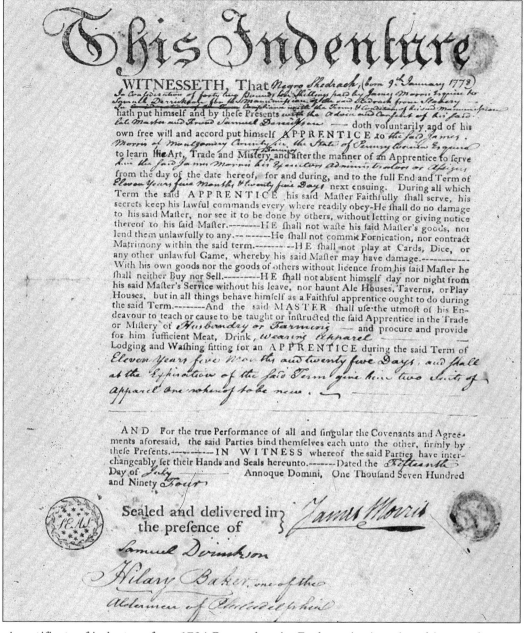

A certificate of indenture from 1794 Pennsylvania. Early on in American history, there was an effort to sign up white indentured servants to work alongside slaves.

One significant outcome of this initial labor system in some southern colonies was that some of the African slaves were granted their freedom in the same manner as the white indentured servants. By 1668, for example, around 30 percent of the slaves who dwelled in Northampton County, Virginia, had been freed. In most cases they obtained paying jobs, and a few came to own their own farms. In what now seems a surprising twist, most of those farm owners purchased their own black slaves to help with the chores.

## Unequal Under the Law

This arrangement did not last long, however, mainly because of large-scale economic factors that were rapidly changing colonial life. First, the number of acres under cultivation in the South greatly expanded, and big cash crops, especially tobacco, became more and more common. These events created a growing need for larger numbers of laborers. To hold down their expenses, planters turned increasingly to the use of slaves, which was the cheapest way to go. The result was a steady increase in the number of black Africans brought into the colonies.

As the number of slaves grew in the late 1600s and early 1700s, white colonial society reacted in part by reducing the already low social status and minimal civil rights that black workers had held. What had been a real chance for Africans to work hard in hopes of gaining their freedom was eliminated by a 1682 Virginia law that made a strong distinction between servants and slaves. Several other colonies soon passed similar statutes, so that thereafter a slave was a slave for life and no different than any other commodity one could buy.

Other laws designed to restrict, dominate, control, and reduce the status of African Americans were created in the years that followed. Prior to the late 1600s, Virginia had allowed the children of a white father and black mother to be free. In 1691, however, the colony enacted a law that ensured that those children would be slaves. Also in 1691 Virginia made it illegal for blacks and whites to intermarry. Other laws made it a crime for a slave to own property, carry a weapon, go out at night without a white person's permission, or leave the slave owner's land without his or her consent.

This trend toward legally limiting the rights of slaves continued at full pace. Extensive collections of laws relating to black slaves—called black codes or slave codes—passed the southern colonial legislatures in the late 1600s and early 1700s. The first one, which appeared in South Carolina in 1696, said in part that the African slaves had "barbarous, wild, savage natures," which "renders them wholly unqualified to be governed by the laws, customs, and practices of this province." So "it is absolutely necessary that such [laws] and [rules] be made and enacted for the good of regulating"[48] and controlling those slaves.

Legally designating African slaves as "barbarous" and "savage" made it possible to categorize them as less than human. White owners and overseers therefore felt perfectly justified in treating their slaves in any manner they saw fit. Some whites continued to treat their black slaves the same way they did their white servants—strictly but with a certain amount of human compassion. More and more slave owners, however, began employing cruel, abusive methods. Some white masters maimed or murdered their slaves at will. In addition, sexual abuse of female slaves by white men became increasingly common and condoned (overlooked) by white males. (Their wives and daughters often realized it was happening and disapproved. But there was usually nothing they could do to stop it.)

To make matters worse, white society passed a spate of laws designed to protect masters who misused their slaves. A 1705 Virginia statute, for example, declared that an owner who killed a slave while disciplining him or her was exempt from prosecution. Similar laws were enacted in other colonies. At the same time, those same colonies passed statutes that called for executing any slave who killed a white person.

## Jefferson's Bold Venture

Thus, by the time that Jefferson was born in Virginia in April 1743, southern colonial American society was, economically speaking, heavily supported by an underclass of legally inferior black slaves. At that time, few slave owners thought for a moment that there was anything unethical about this system. Nevertheless, as the young educated men of Jefferson's generation grew up, some increasingly felt the influence of the European Enlightenment. This was an intellectual movement that advocated a number of basic, noble concepts, including religious toleration and certain fundamental human rights like liberty and freedom of speech.

In particular, Jefferson and other young Americans took to heart many of the precepts of English philosopher John Locke (1632–1704). One of these stated that a natural law of reason taught humanity "that, being equal and independent, no one ought to harm another in his life, health, liberty, or possessions."[49] This and other arguments of the Enlightenment thinkers made it clear that slavery was in and of itself corrupt and unworthy of educated individuals.

Because of such ideas, some colonial Americans came to view slavery as wrong. But two factors kept most of them from doing anything about it. First, they were still in the minority. Second, the institution was so economically and legally entrenched that they did not see a realistic way of eliminating it in a timely fashion.

Then in the 1770s came the sudden creation of the United States, a nation based on the concept of liberty. To Jefferson, this seemed a perfect opportunity to rid America of slavery. To this end, when called upon to write the initial draft of the Declaration of Independence, he included a clause calling for the abolition of the slave trade. He knew that slavery could not be eradicated all at once, so he opted for banning the slave trade first. Getting rid of the institution itself would hopefully come later. (In 1784 he pushed for passage of a law that would have eradicated slavery in all the states, but the U.S. Congress voted it down.) His anti–slave trade clause in the Declaration said in part: "[The English king] has waged cruel war against human nature itself, violating its most sacred rights of life and liberty in the persons of a dis-

*Although a slave owner himself, Thomas Jefferson led the movement to abolish the American slave trade.*

tant people who never offended him [i.e., black Africans], captivating and carrying them into slavery in another hemisphere, or to incur miserable death in their transportation [across the Atlantic]."[50]

Jefferson was mightily disappointed when the Continental Congress rejected the inclusion of these words in the nation's founding document. His attack on the slave trade shocked most of the

That "Peculiar Institution": Slavery in America ■ 69

# Announcing the Arrival of New Slaves

Much evidence of white contempt for black Africans in colonial America has survived. Some of it consists of written depictions in newspapers and on posters of blacks as subhuman or as mere property. For example, an ad in the June 6, 1763, issue of Rhode Island's *Newport Gazette* described some newly arrived Africans, saying, "On Thursday last arrived from the coast of Africa, the brig *Royal Charlotte* with a parcel of extremely fine, healthy, well-limbed Gold Coast slaves—men, women, boys, and girls. Gentlemen in town and country have now an opportunity to furnish themselves with such [slaves] as will suit them. [The slaves] are to be seen [and inspected] on the vessel at Taylor's wharf."

Quoted in Hugh Thomas. *The Slave Trade: The Story of the Atlantic Slave Trade, 1440–1870.* New York: Simon and Schuster, 1997, p. 431.

delegates from the southern states, which were highly dependent on the trade. However, several other delegates were heartened by Jefferson's bold venture against slavery. A generation later, they and others who agreed with them carried the day when in 1807 the U.S. Congress voted to eliminate the slave trade.

## A Wedge Between South and North

When that fateful vote was taken, Jefferson was in the last months of his second term as the third president of the United States. He hoped to see the end of slavery itself in his lifetime. But that was not to be. When he passed away on July 4, 1826, the nation was still in the grip of that awful system of human bondage.

As a result, over the course of the next three decades, slaves in the United States continued to suffer innumerable indignities and brutalities. In addition to the horror and humiliation of being enslaved in the first place, numerous slaves were beaten, tortured, and/or sexually abused by their masters. Moreover, those slave owners were almost never punished for these acts. By the 1850s roughly 3.5 million black slaves lived and worked in the American South. Although only around one in four families in the region had slaves, most southerners came to benefit indirectly from slave labor.

During these decades, the abolitionist groups that had fought so hard to end the slave trade turned their considerable wrath and resources on the institution of slavery itself. While they lectured, wrote pamphlets and books, and worked to free slaves when possible, slavery steadily became a political and social wedge that increasingly separated southern society from the northern states, which had few or no slaves.

In the ongoing debate over the issue, southern whites passionately defended slavery, partly because they felt it was their right to own slaves. They also upheld slavery because cotton was by far the number one crop the South produced. The cotton industry, as it was then run, was thoroughly dependent on slave labor. Huge amounts of cotton had to be picked, and planters believed that paying workers to do it would have greatly reduced or even eliminated profits. Moreover, extremely little heavy industry, then the main profit-making alternative to agriculture, existed in the South. So there was a widespread notion among southerners that if they lost their slaves, the South's economy would collapse.

Still another popular justification for slavery in the South was moral in nature. It held that slave owners had rescued black Africans from a primitive state by enslaving them in America. The owners had done blacks the favor of providing them with food, clothes, and safety, the argument went. Otherwise, black people would be reduced to savagery, since they were barbarous by nature. An influential southerner named Charles C. Burr said, "The Negro, when a 'slave' to a Caucasian, is vastly higher in the scale of humanity than when in his native state."[51]

*Slaves in the United States suffered innumerable indignities and brutalities. In addition to the horror and humiliation of being enslaved, numerous slaves were beaten, tortured, and/ or sexually abused by their masters.*

# Moving Toward War

The abolitionists countered these proslavery arguments with some strong antislavery arguments of their own. First, a number of deeply religious northerners said that all human beings were equal in God's sight and that black people's souls were no less valuable than those of whites. In their view, slavery was both a sin and an affront to God. Slavery was also horribly cruel, abolitionists and other opponents declared. Not only were slaves regularly abused, but slave couples and families were often torn apart when, for example, a master sold a slave's mate or child to another master, often in another state.

Another antislavery argument held that the institution was anti-American. According to this argument, the United States had been founded on the principles of equality, liberty, and justice, and the southern slaves had none of these. A similar argument was voiced in the 1850s by the well-known northern politician William Henry Seward. Slavery was "incompatible with all the elements of the security, welfare, and greatness of nations,"[52] he asserted. So the United States would never become a truly great country until it did away with the ugly stain of slavery.

The differing opinions and impassioned debates concerning the slavery issue continued for many years with no clear agreement or resolution in sight. It was the effort to expand slavery into U.S. territories where it did not yet exist that finally put members of the two sides on a path toward violent confrontation. In the 1840s some U.S. congressmen tried to ban slavery in New Mexico, California, and other western territories. But the bill did not pass. This came as a relief to many southerners who feared becoming a powerless minority in the United States as more nonslavery states joined the union.

Those same proslavery advocates were delighted when the Kansas-Nebraska Act passed in 1854. It granted U.S. territories the authority to determine through popular sovereignty whether or not slavery would be permitted. The act allowed slavery to flourish in the newly created Kansas Territory. In turn, that ignited a round of bloody fighting as pro- and antislavery groups clashed in Kansas. Those who supported slavery in the territories went on a rampage and nearly destroyed the antislavery town of Lawrence, Kansas, in May 1856. In response, antislavery forces demonstrated and rioted in many parts of the North.

Many other violent incidents motivated by the slavery issue occurred in the four years that followed. But none moved the South and North closer to a full-scale war over slavery than the one perpetrated by John Brown in 1859. A fanatical abolitionist, he and his equally zealous sons had gone to Kansas in the mid-1850s and taken part in the fighting that had erupted there. After that, feeling that the continued existence of slavery should not be tolerated, Brown conceived a plan that he hoped would help the slaves free themselves. As scholar

# Subject to Her Master's Will

Sexual abuse of female slaves by white males was common in the nineteenth-century United States. An escaped slave, Harriet Jacobs, who used the pen name Linda Brent, described her own experiences in her 1861 book *Incidents in the Life of a Slave Girl*.

My master began to whisper foul words in my ear. Young as I was, I could not remain ignorant of their import. . . . He peopled my young mind with unclean images, such as only a vile monster could think of. I turned from him with disgust and hatred. But he was my master. I was compelled to live under the same roof with him—where I saw a man forty years my senior daily violating the most sacred commandments of nature. He told me I was his property; that I must be subject to his will in all things.

Linda Brent. *Incidents in the Life of a Slave Girl*. Part 1. FullBooks.com. www.fullbooks.com/Incidents-in-the -Life-of-a-Slave-Girl1.html.

*Escaped slave Harriet Jacobs related her own experiences as a slave in her 1861 book* Incidents in the Life of a Slave Girl.

---

William M.S. Rasmussen of the Virginia Historical Society tells it:

In October 1859, John Brown and twenty-one followers gained armed possession of the federal arsenal at Harpers Ferry, Virginia. Their intent was to confiscate rifles stored there and with those weapons initiate a massive slave insurrection that would spread throughout the South and eventually free all of the nation's four million slaves. Brown, who had plotted the raid for decades, was driven by religious fervor. He believed himself chosen by God for the mission.[53]

The raid, which took place on October 16, 1859, was a failure. Brown and his accomplices were captured, and soon afterward Brown was tried and hung. But he had succeeded in doing damage in ways he had not anticipated. People across the South were enraged, and some believed that an army of escaped

*John Brown's raid on Harper's Ferry, Virginia, and his subsequent arrest and execution, ignited heated sentiments about the issue of slavery in America.*

# A House Divided

A braham Lincoln did not at first advocate the idea of freeing the slaves. But by 1858 he believed that the ongoing expansion of slavery had become dangerous to American unity. In accepting the Republican nomination for the Senate in June of that year, he made the following now famous statement. "A house divided against itself cannot stand. I believe this government cannot endure, permanently half *slave* and half *free*. . . . It will become *all* one thing or *all* the other. Either the *opponents* of slavery will arrest the further spread of it . . . or its *advocates* will push it forward, till it shall become alike lawful in *all* the States."

Abraham Lincoln. "House Divided Speech." Abraham Lincoln Online. http://showcase.netins.net/web /creative/lincoln/speeches/house.htm.

slaves was about to invade the southern states. Even when they found that it was only a rumor, many of them started openly discussing the option of seceding (officially withdrawing) from the Union.

## An Appalling Legacy

The following year, after a succession of other tense moments and violent incidents had transpired, the southern states *did* secede, setting in motion the American Civil War. Historians agree that it had numerous causes. But slavery was the principal one by far. In all, more than six hundred thousand Americans died in the conflict, which lasted from 1861 to 1865.

Since slavery had been the main cause of the war, the federal government found it crucial to address its official abolition as swiftly as possible. Among other things, the government forced the leaders of the southern states to ratify the U.S. Constitution's Thirteenth Amendment, which abolished slavery throughout the United States. The Fourteenth and Fifteenth Amendments, which guaranteed the former slaves equal protection under the law and voting rights, were adopted soon afterward.

To the regret of African Americans across the country, however, the Fourteenth and Fifteenth Amendment reforms turned out to be largely on paper. Truly, slavery no longer existed in the United States. But most white southerners still saw blacks as inferiors and were not willing to afford them all the civil rights due them. This attitude led to a long period of deliberate, unashamed discrimination that lasted for almost a century. Black Americans were socially segregated; denied many rights, often including voting rights;

frequently bullied and/or terrorized; and sometimes even killed.

The civil rights acts passed by the U.S. Congress in the 1950s and 1960s began to erase the appalling legacy of American slavery. Yet the story of human slavery was not over. Some of the people who were happy to see American blacks accorded some degree of justice sadly recognized that slaves still existed throughout the world. Clearly, the self-appointed, centuries-long struggle of the abolitionists was not over.

# Chapter Six

# Slavery's Survival in the Modern World

Today, when asked what they know about slavery, many Americans correctly describe it as a case of one person owning another. But when asked when it last existed, they most often say a hundred or two hundred years ago. According to Boston University scholar Ricco Siasoco, "Most Americans believe slavery was abolished" at the end of the American Civil War "more than a century ago." However, the truth is that "the horrors of human beings held in bondage flourishes today"[54] in many places in the world. Moreover, the United States is one of those places.

Indeed, those Americans who have heard the results of a number of studies of modern slavery have been shocked. "Slavery is a problem the public thinks we solved long ago," remarks Laurel Fletcher, a researcher at the Human Rights Center at the University of California. "But in fact, it's alive and well. It has simply taken on a new form."[55] That

form is generally referred to as human trafficking or trafficking in persons.

## Definition and Scope of Human Trafficking

Experts agree that human trafficking differs somewhat from traditional chattel slavery. In the latter, a person outright owns another, sometimes legally, whereas a human trafficker lures a person into a situation in which the person is exploited but not actually owned. For a good, clear definition of human trafficking, a researcher at the Johns Hopkins University School of Advanced International Studies states that it is

> more subtle than outright slavery ... in that it does not necessarily entail ownership of a person. But rather [it] allows the perpetrators to exert control by insidious means such as threats, coercion, and deception. Crucially, it is the exploitation of

another's vulnerability, whether economic, social, or political, that forms the cornerstone of [human] trafficking. . . . Conditions such as war, displacement, relative income inequality across regions and countries, demand for cheap labor or services, and widespread corruption contribute to [it], creating fertile ground in which trafficking thrives. Trafficking in persons affects men, women, and children, though women and children are most frequently victimized. Trafficking involves the movement of these persons from their place of origin to elsewhere in their communities, provinces, regions, or across countries and continents, to destinations where they are ultimately exploited.[56]

It is important to point out that some of those who are exploited by traffickers are paid for their work. But these are not normal wages in any sense. First, the trafficker often gives victims some money up front in order to entice them to get involved. Once the individuals are hooked, the payments frequently stop. In some cases payments do continue, but they are tiny and never enough to live on.

Instead, these so-called wages are a ploy designed to persuade victims to keep working long hours in virtual servitude as well as often dangerous conditions. The exploited individuals usually fear that if they refuse to work or try to leave, the payments—however small—

will stop. The individuals will then be destitute and lost. This is because in most cases, the trafficker brings victims to a foreign land where the language and culture are alien to them. The workers worry that if they end up on the street in that strange society, they will be arrested, thrown into jail, and forgotten. So as miserable as they are, they stay and continue working for the trafficker, seeing themselves trapped in an impossible situation.

According to the modern studies that have shocked some Americans and others around the world, the scope of human trafficking is nothing short of colossal. Those studies, conducted between the mid-1990s and the present by the U.S. Department of State, the United Nations, and various American and international universities, have given widely varying estimates for the number of people enslaved. The lowest estimates say that 27 million people are slaves at any given time around the globe. The highest estimate claims the number is much larger—at least 200 million. Even if the lowest estimate is more accurate, it is a frightening figure. Consider that 27 million is nearly three times the number of slaves experts think were involved in the Atlantic slave trade over the course of some three centuries.

The studies also show that one reason so many people are now enslaved is that generally, both the cost of buying a slave and the profit from selling one are far less than they were in prior ages. In 1850 the average cost of a slave in the American South was equivalent to

The U.S. State Department, the United Nations, and various American and international universities have given widely varying estimates of the number of people enslaved in the modern world. The lowest estimates say that about 27 million people are slaves at any given time around the globe.

forty thousand dollars in today's money. Today, the average cost of a slave is a mere ninety dollars. Modern slaves are cheap because they are plentiful, highly disposable, and easily replaced by more victims.

## Modern Sex Trafficking

Several varieties or categories of human trafficking exist. The biggest, according to the experts, is sex services and prostitution, which accounts for about 46 percent of modern slavery. It is estimated that the number of young girls forced to become sex slaves is ten times higher than the number of African slaves transported each year in the old Atlantic slave trade. The State Department offers a legal definition for sex trafficking: "When an adult is coerced, forced, or deceived into prostitution, or maintained in prostitution through coercion, that person is a victim of trafficking. All of those involved in recruiting, transporting, harboring, receiving, or obtaining the person for that purpose have committed a trafficking crime."[57]

The words *deceived into prostitution* in the definition are crucial in understanding how this form of slavery works. The victims are frequently lured by various promises made by traffickers posing as photographers, model agency managers, nightclub owners, or other reputable businesspersons. Thinking she is going to become a legitimate model, dancer, or whatever, a young woman (or, somewhat less often, a young man) meets the trafficker in another city. At this point, she suddenly finds that she has been misled and must perform sexual acts on

*Indian sex workers hide their identities at a protest. Victims are frequently lured by various promises made by traffickers posing as photographers, model agency managers, nightclub owners, or other reputable businesspersons.*

a regular basis for little or no money. In some of the poorest nations of Asia and Africa, it is also common for parents to make some badly needed cash by selling their child to a sex trafficker.

While working for the trafficker, the sex slave almost always lives in a small, filthy, single room along with other women or girls trapped in the same dire circumstances. They are all regularly exposed to sexually transmitted diseases such as HIV/AIDs, which some of them contract. The women or girls are kept submissive through fear. Complaining or trying to leave is punished by beatings or worse. The traffickers also keep the slaves in line by threatening to turn them over to the police or to harm their families back home.

Typical is the story of Srey Pov, a young Cambodian girl whose parents sold her to a brothel (house of prostitution) when she was six. She knew nothing about sex at the time and her first introduction to it was through several adult men, all Western tourists, raping her. She was forced to be with up to twenty men a day and later said, "I was so scared. I was crying and asking, 'Why are you doing this to me?'"[58]

The terrified young girl attempted to escape several times. But each time she was quickly caught and severely punished. Sometimes her boss beat her, other times he subjected her to electric shocks, and when these methods did not end her escape attempts, she suffered a fiendish penalty commonly used in Asian brothels. It consists of placing the person in a barrel filled with sew-age that comes up to her chest, sealing it, and leaving her there for hours or even days. The barrel also contains scorpions that repeatedly sting her.

Eventually, the punishments worked, and Srey Pov stopped trying to get away. As a *New York Times* reporter who later interviewed her wrote, "Most girls who have been trafficked, whether in New York or in Cambodia, eventually surrender. They are degraded and terrified, and they doubt their families or society will accept them again."[59] Fortunately for Srey Pov, she made it back to society, which did accept her. When she was nine she was rescued and ended up in a shelter run by an antitrafficking activist who herself had been forced into a brothel as a child.

## Domestic Slavery

The second-most common form of modern slavery is the exploitation of domestic workers, which accounts for roughly 27 percent of human trafficking. Affecting mainly women, it is a growing problem in the United States. Every year thousands of women travel to America from foreign countries either without proper documents or using temporary visas. They think they will be working in high-paying positions as maids, cooks, or other domestics for decent, well-to-do families. Often they come from poor families back home and intend to work for a given length of time in America in order to send part of their salaries back to their needy families.

What happens instead is that the victims are trapped and exploited by traffickers. These criminals force them to become live-in domestics who often work up to nineteen hours a day for little or no money and who are never allowed to leave the house. There they are subject to threats, beatings, and sometimes sexual abuse as well.

These house slaves frequently have few means of remedying their situations. If they are undocumented, they are illegal immigrants, so if they go to the authorities they will likely be deported (sent back to their home country). Even those workers who have visas are not much better off. Their documents are employment based, which means they must continue working for their employer or else be deported. The result is that few of the victims dare to report what is happening to them.

Under these conditions, most of the domestic slaves feel powerless to stop the abuses they suffer. According to Stephen Lendman of the Montreal-based Center for Research on Globalization, these abuses include

> assault and battery, including physical beatings and threats of serious harm; limited freedom of movement, including arbitrary and enforced loss of liberty by use of locks, bars, confiscation of passports and travel documents, chains, and threats of retaliation against other family members; health and safety issues, including unhealthy sleeping situations in basements, utility rooms, or other unsatisfactory places; unsafe working conditions endangering health;

denial of food or proper nutrition; and refusal to provide medical care and having to work when ill.[60]

## Other Kinds of Trafficking

Up to 10 percent of modern slaves are the victims of another form of trafficking—forced agricultural work. Like domestic slaves, those who toil on farms contribute to a growing problem in the United States. Most, though certainly not all, of the nearly 2 million in their ranks live and work in Florida and other southern states, according to a prominent American social research group. These exploited individuals, the group reports, exist in "sub-poverty misery," with little pay, "without benefits, [and] without the right to overtime."[61]

The growers who exploit these workers are motivated by offers for their crops from big food companies. Because the companies demand that the crops be sold to them dirt cheap, the growers try to cut corners by using workers who can be forced to work for little or nothing. Lendman explains:

> The commercial power of giant buyers and retailers like Wal-Mart (selling 19% of US groceries) and Yum Brands (the world's largest fast-food company) squeeze growers and suppliers for the lowest prices. Increased competition from imports have had a similar effect, especially in winter months. Yet while wages and prices to producers are squeezed, profits are

*At this site in the United Kingdom, three men and one woman were arrested for holding a number of people against their will and forcing them to work; some had been held for as long as fifteen years.*

passed up the distribution chain to corporate giants at the top.[62]

Meanwhile, the corrupt growers who exploit the workers most often get away with it, in part because enforcement by state and federal officials is frequently lax. Few questionable growers are investigated, and even fewer are ever prosecuted. Also, few of the laborers, who are often guarded by armed thugs to make sure they cannot run away, ever report their predicaments for fear of losing their jobs. As one of them told an undercover investigator, "If we don't work, we don't eat."[63]

Of the rest of the victims of human trafficking, some work in sweatshops and factories. There they make clothes, carpets, and hundreds of other everyday products, often in dirty, uncomfortable, and dangerous conditions. Others are maids in hotels, and still others cook or bus tables in restaurants. One thing that they and all other modern slaves have in common is that they usually feel trapped and hopeless, believing that society cannot or will not help them.

# The Worst Forms of Child Labor

One of the more menacing forms of modern slavery is the forced labor of children. The U.S. Department of State says the following about child trafficking:

> There is a growing consensus . . . that the worst forms of child labor should be eradicated. The sale and trafficking of children and their entrapment in bonded and forced labor are among these worst forms of child labor. A child can be a victim of human trafficking regardless of the location of that exploitation. Indicators of forced labor of a child include situations in which the child appears to be in the custody of a non-family member who has the child perform work that financially benefits someone outside the child's family and does not offer the child the option of leaving. . . . When children are enslaved, their abusers should not escape criminal punishment.

U.S. Department of State. "What Is Modern Slavery?" www.state.gov/j/tip/what/index.htm.

*The sale and trafficking of children into forced labor is the darkest side of child labor.*

*The United Nations has taken the lead in fighting human trafficking. In 2000, the organization adopted its Trafficking Protocol, which by 2012 had been signed by 117 nations.*

## Antitrafficking Groups and Initiatives

In reality, some help for the victims of human trafficking has been forthcoming. On an international scale, the United Nations has taken the lead. In 2000 the organization adopted its Trafficking Protocol, which by 2012 had been signed by 117 nations. Backed by United Nations funding, this international agreement helps governments draft antitrafficking laws and create strategies to fight traffickers. A similar effort, the Council of Europe Convention on Action Against Trafficking in Human Beings, was adopted by most European nations in 2005.

In the United States, meanwhile, a number of laws were passed in the 1990s that prohibit human trafficking. These were reinforced by a sweeping 2000 statute called the Victims of Trafficking and Violence Protection Act (VTVPA). It allocated money for research into the modern slavery problem, investigations and prosecutions of traffickers, and legal aid and other assistance for victims. The VTVPA also set prison terms for convicted traffickers of up to twenty years or longer.

In addition, several U.S. agencies deal with human trafficking, either directly or indirectly. Two of these, established by the VTVPA, are the Office to Monitor and

Combat Trafficking in Persons and the President's Interagency Task Force. Also, the State Department's Bureau of Population, Refugees, and Migration and the U.S. Department of Health and Human Services (HHS) have programs to identify, help, and protect victims of modern slavery. A trafficking hotline run by the HHS has taken more than fifty thousand calls and provided law enforcement agencies with some three thousand tips about trafficking operations. Also ongoing are efforts by the U.S. Department of Justice to prosecute traffickers.

Private U.S. antitrafficking groups have also been established in recent years. They include, among others, Stop Trafficking, Not for Sale, the Polaris Project, Compassion2One, and End Slavery Now. Also, a growing number of well-to-do private companies and individuals have contributed money to the effort to stop human trafficking. In 2011, for example, the Internet giant Google donated $11.5 million to ongoing efforts to fight human trafficking. Similarly, in 2012 seventeen Major League Baseball players, from eight separate teams, pledged to give a portion of their salaries to a new initiative launched by Not for Sale.

## "We Must Do More"

Despite the recent efforts of all of these international and U.S. agencies and private

## Some Modern-Day Abolitionists

One of the most active modern anti–human trafficking organizations—the Polaris Project—describes its abolitionist mission in the following manner:

Polaris Project is one of the leading organizations in the global fight against human trafficking and modern-day slavery. Named after the North Star "Polaris" that guided slaves to freedom along the Underground Railroad, Polaris Project is transforming the way that individuals and communities respond to human trafficking, in the U.S. and globally.

By successfully pushing for stronger federal and state laws, operating the National Human Trafficking Resource Center hotline (1-888-373-7888), conducting trainings, and providing vital services to victims of trafficking, Polaris Project creates long-term solutions that move our society closer to a world without slavery.

Polaris Project. "About Polaris Project." www.polarisproject.org/about-us/overview.

organizations, experts agree that only a small dent has been made so far in worldwide human trafficking. For example, a 2012 report by the U.S. Congress's public policy research group, the Congressional Research Service, stated: "Despite U.S. and international efforts, perpetrators continue to persist in victimizing men, women, and children worldwide through commercial sexual exploitation, forced labor, [and other kinds of trafficking]."[64]

This and other recent reports by expert observers generally agree on why progress in the fight against human trafficking has been relatively small. First and foremost, the scope of the problem is huge. The tens of thousands of traffickers and tens of millions of victims are spread around the globe. Most of the traffickers are well funded, smart, and well trained in avoiding both the police and legal prosecution. To overcome these strengths requires enormous amounts of money, time, and human resources, and to date, all of these commodities have been too limited. Second, most law enforcement agencies in the world that are trained to fight trafficking are still fairly new. So they have not yet been as successful as they would like in coordinating their efforts.

Yet the same observers who have been critical of antitrafficking efforts are also confident that over time those efforts will continue to gain momentum. The many people who have joined the antitrafficking ranks in recent years are earnest, dedicated, and willing to see the fight through until it is won. One of these committed individuals, Harold Koh, a legal adviser to the State Department, remarked in 2011:

We must do more to help close [the] gaps [that exist in our anti-trafficking efforts], both at home and abroad. So long as anyone toils as a victim of trafficking in the United States, Asia or elsewhere, [we] will continue to fight this plague wherever it arises. In the 21st Century, it is long past time for us to stop tolerating this kind of lawless global abuse of our fellow human beings![65]

# Notes

## Introduction: How Historians Learn About Slavery

1. Richard C. Carrier. "The Function of the Historian in Society." *History Teacher*, August 2002, p. 519.
2. John Noble Wilford. "At Burial Site, Teeth Tell Tale of Slavery." *New York Times*, January 31, 2006. www.nytimes.com/2006/01/31/science/31slav.html?pagewanted=2.
3. Quoted in Livius.org. *The Epic of Atrahasis*. Translated by Benjamin R. Foster. www.livius.org/as-at/atrahasis/atrahasis.html.
4. Quoted in Naphtali Lewis and Meyer Reinhold, eds. *Roman Civilization: Sourcebook II; The Empire*. New York: Harper and Row, 1966, p. 280.
5. Keith Bradley. *Slavery and Society at Rome*. Cambridge: Cambridge University Press, 1994, pp. 179–180.

## Chapter One: Slavery in the Earliest Civilizations

6. Hugh Thomas. *The Slave Trade*. New York: Simon and Schuster, 1997, p. 25.
7. Bamber Gascoigne. "History of Slavery." History World. www.historyworld.net/wrldhis/PlainTextHistories.asp?historyid=ac41.
8. Daniel C. Snell. *Life in the Ancient Near East, 3100–332 B.C.* New Haven, CT: Yale University Press, 1998, p. 66.
9. Ancient History Sourcebook. "Code of Hammurabi." Translated by L.W. King. www.fordham.edu/halsall/ancient/hamcode.asp.
10. Quoted in Karl Müller. *Geographi Graeci Minores*. Hildesheim, Germany: Olms, 1990, pp. 124, 127.
11. Quoted in Kautilya. *The Arthashastra*. Indian History Sourcebook. www.fordham.edu/halsall/india/kautilya1.asp#Book%20III,%20Chapter%2013.
12. Charles Benn. *Daily Life in Traditional China: The Tang Dynasty*. Westport, CT: Greenwood, 2002, p. 39.
13. Keith Bradley and Paul Cartledge, eds. *The Cambridge World History of Slavery*. Vol. 1. New York: Cambridge University Press, 2011, p. 3.

## Chapter Two: Slavery Defined as Natural: Ancient Greece

14. Pseudo-Xenophon (or the "Old Oligarch"). *Constitution of the Athenians*. In Xenophon, *Scripta Minora*, translated by E.C. Marchant. Cambridge, MA: Harvard University Press, 1993, p. 481.
15. Antiphon. *On the Murder of Herodes*. In *The Murder of Herodes and Other Trials from the Athenian Law Courts*,

edited by Kathleen Freeman. New York: Norton, 1963, p. 74.

16. Plutarch. "Life of Lycurgus." In *Plutarch on Sparta*, translated by Richard J.A. Talbert. New York: Penguin, 1988, p. 41.

17. Xenophon. *Oeconomicus*. In *Xenophon: Conversations of Socrates*, translated by Hugh Tredennick and Robin Waterfield. New York: Penguin, 1990, p. 323.

18. Xenophon. *Oeconomicus*, p. 326.

19. Robert Flaceliere. *Daily Life in Greece at the Time of Pericles*. Translated by Peter Green. London: Phoenix, 1996, p. 50.

20. Aristotle. *Athenian Constitution*. Translated by H. Rackham. Cambridge, MA: Harvard University Press, 1996, p. 139.

21. Aristotle. *Politics*. Translated by J.A. Sinclair. Baltimore: Penguin, 1962, p. 74.

22. Aristotle. *Politics*, 94.

23. Xenophon. *Oeconomicus*, p. 334.

24. Quoted in Thomas Wiedemann, ed. *Greek and Roman Slavery*. Baltimore: Johns Hopkins University Press, 1981, p. 47.

25. Quoted in Wiedemann. *Greek and Roman Slavery*, p. 47.

## Chapter Three: Slavery on an Immense Scale: Ancient Rome

26. Quoted in Wiedemann. *Greek and Roman Slavery*, pp. 15, 24.

27. Bradley. *Slavery and Society at Rome*, pp. 25–26.

28. Matthew Bunson. *Dictionary of the Roman Empire*. New York: Oxford University Press, 1991, p. 391.

29. P.A. Brunt. *Social Conflicts in the Roman Republic*. New York: Norton, 1971, p. 18.

30. L.P. Wilkinson. *The Roman Experience*. Lanham, MD: University Press of America, 1974, p. 128.

31. Lucius Junius Columella. *On Agriculture*. Vol. 1. Translated by H.B. Ash et al. Cambridge, MA: Harvard University Press, 1960, p. 85.

32. Plutarch. "Life of Crassus." In *Plutarch: Fall of the Roman Republic,* translated by Rex Warner. New York: Penguin, 1972, p. 122.

33. Quoted in Wiedemann. *Greek and Roman Slavery*, p. 192.

34. Quoted in Keith Hopkins. *Conquerors and Slaves: Sociological Studies in Roman History*. Vol. 1. New York: Cambridge University Press, 1978, p. 121.

35. Quoted in Wiedemann. *Greek and Roman Slavery*, p. 194.

36. Quoted in Wiedemann. *Greek and Roman Slavery*, p. 190.

## Chapter Four: The Early Modern Slave Trade Develops

37. Michael Grant. *A Social History of Greece and Rome*. New York: Scribner's, 1992, pp. 90–91.

38. Gascoigne. "History of Slavery."

39. S.I. Martin. "Slavery in Africa." Antislavery International. http://old.antislavery.org/breakingthe silence/slave_routes/slave_routes_portugal.shtml.

40. Johannes Postma. *The Atlantic Slave Trade*. Westport, CT: Greenwood, 2005, p. 10.

41. Arthur Gonineau. *The Inequality of Human Races*. Translated by Adrian Collins. New York: Putnam, 1915, pp. 205–210.

42. Olaudah Equiano. *Equiano's Travels.* Edited by Paul Edwards. Oxford: Heinemann, 1996, p. 24.

43. Quoted in Howard Zinn. *A People's History of the United States*. New York: HarperCollins, 2005, p. 28.
44. Quoted in Thomas Howard, ed. *Black Voyage: Eyewitness Accounts of the Atlantic Slave Trade*. Boston: Little, Brown, 1971, pp. 206–208.

## Chapter Five: That "Peculiar Institution": Slavery in America

45. The answer to the question of why Jefferson did not free all of his own slaves is complicated and often debated. An informative discussion of the issue can be found in noted researcher David Barton's thoughtful article "George Washington, Thomas Jefferson, and Slavery in America," available at www.wallbuilders.com/libissuesarticles.asp?id=99.
46. Thomas Jefferson. "The Declaration of Independence." In *The Democracy Reader*, edited by Diane Ravitch and Abigail Thernstrom. New York: HarperCollins, 1992, p. 101.
47. Zinn. *A People's History of the United States*, p. 25.
48. Quoted in John B. Boles. *Black Southerners, 1619–1869*. Lexington: University Press of Kentucky, 1985, p. 23.
49. John Locke. *The Second Treatise of Government*. Edited by Thomas P. Peardon. Indianapolis: Bobbs-Merrill, 1952, p. 4.
50. Quoted in Carl Becker. *The Declaration of Independence: A Study in the History of Political Ideas*. New York: Harcourt, Brace, 1922, pp. 212–213.
51. Quoted in Stephen G. Hyslop. *Eyewitness to the Civil War*. Washington, DC: National Geographic, 2006, p. 24.
52. Quoted in George E. Baker, ed. *The Works of William H. Seward*. Vol. 4. New York: AMS, 1972, pp. 291–292.
53. William M.S. Rasmusen and Robert S. Tilton. "The Portent: John Brown's Raid in American Memory." Virginia Historical Society. www.vahistorical.org/johnbrown/introduction.htm.

## Chapter Six: Slavery's Survival in the Modern World

54. Ricco Siasoco. "Modern Slavery: Human Bondage in Africa, Asia, and the Dominican Republic." Fact Monster, April 18, 2001. www.factmonster.com/spot/slavery1.html.
55. Quoted in Janet Gilmore. "Modern Slavery Thriving in the U.S." UC Berkeley NewsCenter, September 23, 2004. http://berkeley.edu/news/media/releases/2004/09/23_16691.shtml.
56. Mohamed Y. Mattar. "Combating Trafficking in Persons in Accordance with the Principles of Islamic Law." United Nations Office on Drugs and Crime. www.unodc.org/documents/human-trafficking/UNODC_Trafficking_and_Islamic_Law_-_Amended.pdf.
57. US Department of State. "What Is Modern Slavery?" www.state.gov/j/tip/what/index.htm.
58. Quoted in Nicholas D. Kristof. "The Face of Modern Slavery." *New York Times*, November 16, 2011. www.nytimes.com/2011/11/17/opinion/kristof-the-face-of-modern-slavery.html?_r=1.
59. Kristof. "The Face of Modern Slavery."
60. Stephen Lendman. "Modern Slavery in America." *Baltimore (MD)*

*Chronicle*, March 6, 2009. http://baltimorechronicle.com/2009/030609Lendman.shtml.

61. Quoted in Lendman. "Modern Slavery in America."
62. Lendman. "Modern Slavery in America."
63. Quoted in Lendman. "Modern Slavery in America."
64. Liana Sun Wyler. "Trafficking in Persons: International Dimension and Foreign Policy Issues for Congress." Congressional Research Service, October 17, 2012. www.fas.org/sgp/crs/row/R42497.pdf.
65. Harold Koh. "Fighting the New Global Slave Trade." White House, May 18, 2011. www.whitehouse.gov/blog/2011/05/18/fighting-new-global-slave-trade.

# Glossary

**abolitionist:** A person who works to end slavery.

**antiquity:** Ancient times.

**black codes (or slave codes):** Collections of laws passed in the early American southern states that severely limited the rights and privileges of black people.

**chattel:** Property; chattel slavery is the outright ownership of one person by another.

*coloni* **(singular is** *colonus***):** In ancient Rome, poor agricultural workers, nicknamed "slaves of the soil," who became dependent on wealthy landowners for work, food, and security.

**commercial slaves:** Slaves who work in shops or other businesses.

**debt bondage:** A kind of slavery in which a person voluntarily enslaves him- or herself long enough to work off a debt.

**domestic slaves:** Slaves who work in homes or other private settings.

**dynasty:** A family line of rulers.

*familia rustica:* In ancient Rome, farm slaves.

**freedman:** A former slave who has been freed; the term *freedwoman* also exists, but more often *freedman* is used to describe both genders.

*fugitivus* **(plural is** *fugitivi***):** In ancient Rome, an escaped slave.

**helots:** The slaves in the ancient Greek city-state of Sparta.

**historic:** Describing periods in history when written records existed.

**human trafficking (or trafficking in persons):** A modern form of slavery in which a person is held against his or her will and exploited but not necessarily owned by the trafficker.

**indentured servant:** In the early modern period, a free person who agreed to work for someone for a set number of months or years in payment for a favor.

**manumission:** The act of freeing one or more slaves.

**neck collar:** A wooden or metal ring placed around a slave's neck to control him or her.

**prehistoric:** Describing periods in history before the advent of written records.

**public slaves:** Slaves who work for the government or on government-sponsored projects.

*servi privati:* In ancient Rome, privately owned slaves who were most often household slaves.

*servi publici:* In ancient Rome, publicly owned slaves who worked for the government.

**sub-Saharan:** Describing areas or peoples located south of Africa's Sahara Desert.

**trans-Saharan:** Describing peoples, trade, or slavery existing in or across Africa's Sahara Desert.

**tribute:** Gifts given by one party to acknowledge submission to another.

*vilicus:* In ancient Rome, a slave assigned by his master to manage the master's farm or estate.

# For More Information

## Books

Anne C. Bailey. *African Voices of the Atlantic Slave Trade*. Boston: Beacon, 2006. A descendant of black slaves examines the Atlantic slave trade through African sources, some of them only recently discovered.

Kevin Bales et al. *Modern Slavery: The Secret World of 27 Million People*. Oxford: Oneworld, 2009. An informative, easy-to-read, sometimes gripping general look at modern human trafficking.

R.H. Barrow. *Slavery in the Roman Empire*. New York: Barnes and Noble, 1996. In one of the better expert overviews of the subject, Barrow quotes extensively from Tacitus, Pliny the Younger, and other ancient writers who discussed slavery.

David Batstone. *Not for Sale: The Return of the Global Slave Trade—and How We Can Fight It*. New York: HarperOne, 2010. A well-researched, at times eye-opening overview of the ravages of modern slavery.

Ira Berlin et al., eds. *Free at Last: A Documentary History of Slavery, Freedom, and the Civil War*. New York: New Press, 2001. This is one of the better collections of primary sources on slavery in the United States before and during the Civil War.

Jeremy Black. *A Brief History of Slavery*. Philadelphia: Running Press, 2011. In language easily understood by general and young adult readers, Black describes slavery in ancient times and how the institution grew to even larger proportions in modern times.

Nigel Bolland. *Struggles for Freedom: Essays on Slavery, Colonialism, and Culture in the Caribbean and Central America*. Belize City, Belize: Angelus, 2005. A collection of essays, each by an expert, exploring various aspects of the transatlantic slave trade.

Rosalie David. *Handbook to Life in Ancient Egypt*. New York: Facts On File, 2008. A handy, easy-to-read compilation of general information about ancient Egyptian society, customs, and people, with a fair amount of space devoted to slaves and slavery.

Basil Davidson, ed. *African Civilization Revisited*. Trenton, NJ: Africa World, 1991. This book uses excerpts of African source materials within a narrative that tells about the role played by Africans in the Atlantic slave trade and how the trade affected African societies.

N.R.E. Fisher. *Slavery in Classical Greece*. London: Bristol Classical Press, 2013. An excellent synopsis of the lives and struggles of Greek slaves.

Michael Grant. *A Social History of Greece and Rome*. New York: Scribner, 1992. This book by the late, popular Grant provides a useful general overview of social relations in the ancient Mediterranean world, including informative chapters on serfs, slaves, and freedmen.

Jason O. Horton and Lois E. Horton. *Slavery and the Making of America*. New York: Oxford University Press, 2006. This excellent book contains up-to-date slavery scholarship and extensive use of slave narratives and archival photos.

Anne Kamma. *If You Lived When There Was Slavery in America*. New York: Scholastic, 2004. Aimed at younger readers, this volume presents the basic facts about what life was like for both slaves and nonslaves in the 1800s.

James McPherson. *Battle Cry of Freedom: The Civil War Era*. New York: Oxford University Press, 2003. Widely seen as the best single-volume history of the Civil War, McPherson's book describes in detail how disagreements about slavery led to that conflict.

Johannes Postma. *The Atlantic Slave Trade*. Westport, CT: Greenwood, 2005. An excellent, easy-to-read overview of the slave trade, with many revealing statistics about the number of slaves shipped from Africa to the Americas.

Daniel C. Snell. *Life in the Ancient Near East, 3100–332 B.C.* New Haven, CT: Yale University Press, 1998. A sweeping overview of ancient Middle Eastern cultures, customs, ideas, and institutions, including slaves and slavery.

## Internet Sources

Ancient History Sourcebook. "Code of Hammurabi." Translated by L.W. King. www.fordham.edu/halsall/ancient/hamcode.asp.

Jimmy Dunn. "Slaves and Slavery in Ancient Egypt." Tour Egypt, October 24, 2011. www.touregypt.net/featurestories/slaves.htm.

Information Britain. "The Iron Age." www.information-britain.co.uk/historydetails/article/27.

Nicholas D. Kristof. "The Face of Modern Slavery." *New York Times*, November 16, 2011. www.nytimes.com/2011/11/17/opinion/kristof-the-face-of-modern-slavery.html?_r=1.

Colin Waugh. "The Haitian Revolution and Atlantic Slavery." *Workers' Liberty*, March 2002. http://archive.workersliberty.org/wlmags/wl102/haiti.htm.

## Websites

**Africans in America, PBS Online** (www.pbs.org/wgbh/aia/part1/1p268.html). Explores the slave era in U.S. history; includes a page that describes several of the laws passed in colonial Virginia to control the blacks brought to the colony by slave traders.

**Polaris Project** (www.polarisproject.org). The main website of one of the most active modern antislavery groups.

**UNODC** (www.unodc.org/unodc/en/human-trafficking/index.html?ref=menuside). A website run by the United Nations Office on Drugs and

Crime that provides excellent information about human trafficking and what can be done to prevent it.

**Wilberforce Central** (www.wilberforcecentral.org/wfc/Wilberforce /index.htm). Contains an excellent, brief overview of the key figure in the abolition of the Atlantic slave trade, as well as links to related topics.

# Index

Crassus, Marcus Licinius, 47

D
Debt slavery, 17–18, 19
Deceived into prostitution, 80–81
Declaration of Independence, 68
Department of Health and
   Human Services, U.S. (HHS),
   86
Department of State, U.S., 78, 84
Domestic slavery, modern,
   81–82

E
Egypt, ancient, 20–21
The Enlightenment, 68
Equiano, Olaudah, 57, *57*, 58–59
Etruscan slavery, 25–26

F
Falconbridge, Alexander, 59
*Familia rustica* (farm slaves), 44
Fifteenth Amendment, 75
Flaceliere, Robert, 31–32
Fletcher, Laurel, 77
Fourteenth Amendment, 75

G
Gascoigne, Bamber, 16, 53
Genoa, 54
Greece, ancient
   acceptance of slavery, 34–37
   domestic slaves in, 30–31

process of becoming freedman
   in, 37–38
public slaves in, 31–34
role of slaves in Athens
   marketplace, 33
types of slaves in, 27–28

H
Hammurabi (Babylonian
   monarch), 19, 20
Harpers Ferry, raid on (1859),
   73–75
Helots (Spartan slaves), 29–30,
   31
HHS (U.S. Department of Health
   and Human Services), 86
Hispaniola, 56
"House Divided Speech"
   (Lincoln), 75
Human trafficking, 11
   definition/scope of, 77–79
   groups/initiatives against,
   85–87

I
*Incidents in the Life of a Slave Girl*
   (Jacobs), 73
Indentured servants, 55, 65
India, 22, 24
Isidorus, C. Caelius, 43
Italy, 25–26

J
Jacobs, Harriet, 73

# Picture Credits

# About the Author

In addition to his acclaimed volumes on the ancient world, historian Don Nardo has produced numerous books about medieval and modern society, including studies of the leading cultural, social, and military aspects of those societies. Besides slavery, these include religious issues, scientific developments, colonialism, terrorism, women's rights, literary trends, the arts, architecture, and the theater. His book *Migrant Mother*, which examines the background of the most iconic photo of the Great Depression, was nominated for eight awards for best book of the year. Nardo, who also composes and arranges orchestral music, lives with his wife, Christine, in Massachusetts.